STOPPING BAD THINGS HAPPENING

TO GOOD SCHOOLS AND GOOD SCHOOL LEADERS

DR MIKE WATERS

First Published 2018

by John Catt Educational Ltd,
12 Deben Mill Business Centre, Old Maltings Approach,
Melton, Woodbridge IP12 1BL

Tel: +44 (0) 1394 389850 Fax: +44 (0) 1394 386893
Email: enquiries@johncatt.com
Website: www.johncatt.com

ISBN: 978 1 909717 54 6

Set and designed by John Catt Educational Limited

Contents

Dedication

To Phil Barnett, Tina Gobell, Robin Hammerton and Helen Jones – all serving or former headteachers of great experience, integrity and wisdom. I thank them all for their assiduous reading of the manuscript and for their comments on it.

Using this book

This book can be used in several ways, depending on what you want from it. You can use it as an *aide memoir* for things you need to do, some of which you may not have previously considered. You can use it as the basis for discussions and decision-making with your senior colleagues. You can also use it as the basis for a set of more formal documents for the school and its future flourishing. There's no one right way to apply the material, but I do provide a series of practical steps and strong suggestions, so you will want to take account of these in a way that suits your situation.

There is logic to the order of presentation, but if you want to take things out of the sequence in which they are presented, or focus upon specific parts that are most immediately salient for you, then of course do so.

You will have noted that the book is short. This is deliberate. I wanted it to be punchy, not a tome. I didn't want to include any more theory or discursive material than absolutely necessary, though there is a little for those who value a degree of stimulation along with the practical advice.

The book lends itself to a first quick read that could almost be done in a single sitting, and then more intensive engagement with the different parts.

After the main body of the book, there are three short chapters written by those who have been through the kinds of 'bad' experiences that the book has been written to address. These bring to life and make very real the situations I talk about. For obvious reasons, they have been written anonymously by headteachers and others who have generously shared what they have been through so that you can try to avoid going through anything similar. There is also a chapter offering the very helpful law-related lessons that one school leader has acquired through her harrowing experiences, plus an appendix.

A note on terms

There are now several terms for those in school leadership roles, including headteacher, head of school, principal, and executive headteacher. Of course, these are different roles and not generally interchangeable titles. For the sake of simplicity, I'm using just two of these terms: headteacher and school leader, the latter of which is a catch-all for all those with leadership responsibilities, including senior leadership team members such as deputy headteachers.

Preface: Setting the Scene

This is not a book I ever planned or wanted to write. Nor was the background to this book – the work I've done with schools and school leaders who have been through distressing and sometimes horrendous experiences – work I ever wanted to do. As little as ten years ago, I couldn't have imagined the situations that some schools now have to go through. It's because of these situations, and the need to address them, that this book has come about.

In some ways, schools now operate in a very different world to the one they did just a decade or so ago – a social media world, for one thing. And it's a world in which schools – along with all kinds of other organisations and a great many individuals – encounter what I've come to call the **dynamics of disproportionality**. This means, in part, molehills so easily becoming mountains. It means people getting outraged about something that many other people would regard as relatively unimportant or just not worth getting worked-up about. For some people, it means escalating an issue as a default response. It means losing all sense of perspective – for example, demanding the school excludes a child for an action well within the normal range of 'children's behaviour'.

It can also mean a disproportionate level of fear: disproportionate to the actual as opposed to the perceived level of risk, as well as the fear of disproportionate consequences. Many school leaders I work with admit that some of their actions are fear-driven and that they operate in a culture of fear. There's the fear of being accused of something, for example, and the fear of being perceived as under-performing. Unfortunately, in today's world, feeling and responding to a degree of fear may be both justified and protective.

The new-ish world in which schools operate is also undoubtedly better in many ways – more open, more responsive to parents and committed to more of a genuine partnership with parents and carers and, in 'power' terms, a more symmetrical relationship than that which tended to obtain in the past. Arguably, though, some of the shock-to-the-system challenges that some schools face nowadays are in part 'enabled' by their desire to be open and accommodating (some might suggest, me included, over-accommodating) to parents and others. This is contentious stuff, but I think it needs to be said.

The starting point for this book is the observation that things can go seriously belly-up for any school and any school leader or, indeed, any teacher, at any time. A sudden crisis, a vexatious allegation, a traumatic and protracted media onslaught – these things can and are bringing turbulence, damage and distress to far too many schools and to school leaders and teachers with otherwise unblemished careers.

Of course, school leaders and others connected with the schools they lead can bring problems on themselves. If they do act in ways which are unprofessional or irresponsible – or even immoral or illegal – then they obviously deserve all that befalls them. If you're a senior leader or teacher in a school and you misrepresent your data, change test papers, siphon funds, intimidate other staff members or have totally inappropriate relationships with members of your staffing establishment or pupil body, then this book won't offer you any escape route. But almost certainly you wouldn't dream of doing any of these things. School leaders don't always act wisely (who does?), but the vast majority seek to do the right things most of the time, and yet they can still find themselves caught up in situations with sometimes devastating consequences. It's with these kinds of situation that this book is concerned. I'm calling them potential **shock-to-the-system**, **school-destabilising** and **school-/personnel-harming** events. I'm using these terms to try to capture the potential seriousness and impact of the precipitating events, not to sound dramatic or create more jargon. The short-hand is just 'bad things'.

They include:

- Allegations and complaints (valid, vexatious and false) taken up, magnified and possibly distorted by the media and social media.
- Scandals and criminal activity involving staff members.
- The sudden suspension, removal or 'disappearance' of a school leader or other senior figure.
- Any critical incident deemed to have been seriously mishandled and so reputation-damaging.
- Serious physical attacks on staff or pupils, including those resulting in serious damage or even death.
- Events requiring emergency evacuations.

This is not an exhaustive list. It doesn't include, for example, serious IT failures and hacks or what for many in education is the most obvious shock-to-the-system event: a damaging (though possibly 'fair') Ofsted inspection, especially one that results in the departure of the headteacher.

I'm not going to say very much directly about the latter, all-too-common situation, so let me say something here that might be proactively helpful.

School leaders: Help yourselves

My explanation for the pushing out of school leaders following a 'bad' Ofsted or poor results more generally is that it too often represents an attribution error on the part of those doing the pushing. That is, the local authority and/or governors or MAT hierarchy over-estimate the significance and impact of the leader in much the same way that Premier League football clubs over-estimate the impact of managers on the performance of their teams.

Headteachers have an impact but it's not all-determining. The 'it's all down to them' (the headteacher) narrative is, however, neat and it simplifies multi-factorial reality to pin everything on the head. It makes for a simple story. It's the story that the Department for Education and Ofsted might be accused of perpetuating. Sometimes, it has to be said, it's a narrative that 'heroic' heads have helped to fashion about themselves. And it is certainly more than possible for school leaders to collaborate in their own demise.

So what's the solution to the attribution error, as I'm characterising it? The solution is to challenge the neat reductionism of that story. It's to point to and explain the attribution error, not as a one-off task but as a continuous process of educating and enlightening those in charge, including governors and trustees. It's to build a compelling and incontestable case over time.

If leadership truly is distributed within a school – and it's down to the head and governors to ensure that it is – then it means also that responsibility is widely distributed and shared, and that no one person can be held responsible for performance failures. It's also up to the leadership team to make sure that all the other many factors that impact on results and other aspects of the school's performance are being identified and foregrounded. All these factors make for a messy story but a much more honest one.

It's the responsibility of the headteacher to demonstrate the actions that s/he has taken to address the negative impact factors, to show that s/he has operated from cause (causing things to happen) rather than from effect (being the passive recipient of other people's actions). The head is then in a much stronger position to resist becoming the 'fall guy' and to systematically dismantle the attribution error that suggests, spuriously of course, that everything is 'down' to him or her. Leaving it to the eleventh hour to challenge the attribution error, when things look seriously bad and the head is already half-way out of the door, is leaving it much too late.

It's up to all other staff members with leadership roles to do the same as their headteachers, and for the latter to make sure that they do.

What else can school leaders do to help themselves?

What school leaders can do is apply the ideas for preventing and preparing for problems that you'll find in the following chapters. But more specifically in relation to 'bad' or disappointing results, which often equate to a drop in achievement for one or more cohort of pupils, they can either take the right, robust action to try to prevent a slump in performance (ideal) or anticipate the drop and prepare for the consequences. If worse-than-previous results are expected (and they often can be, especially during times of significant alterations to examinations and assessment processes) then the key is to be very clear about the measures taken to try to address the factors responsible.

Make sure that parents and governors/trustees are given clear information about the contextual factors and the actions taken. Arguably, the best time to do this is while the pupils are preparing for the tests, not after they've taken them. It is also important to identify as precisely as possible the specific reasons for the comparatively poor results, assuming that the preventative measures weren't sufficient to avoid the worst. Everyone in the school should sing from the same hymn sheet. It's the responsibility of the leadership team to ensure they do.

The poor results that school leaders dread and know can make their tenure vulnerable might not in themselves precipitate a push to the exit. But what relatively poor results can do is ferment unrest, aggravate an already negative climate or play into the hands of those looking for a pretext to do some 'house-clearing'. Indeed, some of the school-destabilising events I refer to in the book have at least some of their roots in the discontent of parents and other stakeholders at regressive test results, especially if they are left unexplained or the explanations don't convince.

Some background

Let's return to the general theme. I hope that what I have to say and the advice I offer will be relevant to many kinds of negative impact events. However, the emphasis will be on the actions and allegations of parents and others, especially those that seem to come out of the blue, spiral out of control or magnify the minor. There are two reasons for making these centre stage. First, because so many of the problems schools experience are indeed precipitated by parents, by other individuals within the school community and/or by the school's response to them (though, of course, the vast majority of parents are supportive and cooperative). Second, because that's where much of my involvement with and support for schools has focused.

A bit of background might be helpful. I've worked with many hundreds of schools, first as a Local Authority adviser/senior adviser and then as an independent consultant, coach and trainer. Most of those schools have, fortunately, never been brought to their knees by bad things happening to them. But some have, and a few years ago one of those schools asked me to help them cope with what they, the Senior Leadership Team (SLT) in particular, were going through, and then to produce some kind of framework that would help them to better cope with any potentially destabilising event they might encounter in the future.

I worked with them on what we called a **Response Management Protocol**. It set out in detail how the school might/should respond to the kinds of events that had already rocked it very badly. So it addressed the question:

How specifically should our school, but maybe all schools/headteachers/ governing bodies, respond when bad things happen?

The school in question – I shall obviously not identify it or any of the other schools I've worked with – found it very useful.

But what I came to realise was that a Response Management Protocol was only one part of what schools and school leaders needed. They needed above all to try to avoid ever having to deal with a school-harming event, so needed to put in place measures to avoid or, more realistically, minimise the chances of bad things occurring and to be ready for them if they did. So they needed a Response Management Plan but also two other strategies or plans:

A **Prevention Management Plan** which addressed the question: *What action can/should we take to minimise the likelihood of a destabilising or shock-to-the-system incident ever happening to us?*

A **Preparation Management Plan** which addressed the question: *What can/should we do to prepare for the possibility of something shocking happening to us?*

What follows covers all three areas: prevention, preparation and response. I've retained the term Response Management Protocol as a useful wrap-around term for all three phases of getting things right.

Some of the material I present formed the basis for training events that I have provided for many different groups of school leaders (heads, deputies and others) including NAHT groups. I have also provided the training for other school staff groups, particularly for those in frequent contact with parents (SENCOs, Family Liaison Officers *etc*) and an appropriately adjusted version for groups of local authority school governors.

I hope you find what follows helpful. Obviously, the suggestions I make are not school-specific and bespoke so may not be (entirely) relevant for situations you may encounter. And there will almost certainly be situations which will not be 'covered', or only partially so, by the guidance I give, and other situations will be governed by school regulations and areas of the law – those pertaining to harassment, for example. It's obviously impossible to design a protocol comprehensive enough to cover every possible scenario. Such a thing would be too hideously complex to be of any practical worth.

Chapter One: What a Response Management Protocol will do for you

Most obviously, the Response Management Protocol (RMP) is an insurance policy. You hope you won't need it, but it's there if you do. But it's not quite an insurance policy because you can't have it and then forget it. The chances are, you will need the prevention plan in place all the time, the preparation plan to operate some of the time and the response plan only occasionally in its entirety or not at all for anything truly serious.

You never know what's going to happen next. What is certain is that the history of a school and its leaders is a poor indicator of its future. Bad things happen to very good schools with excellent and thoroughly deserved reputations and track records. Indeed, my experience has been that the worst shocks seem to happen to the 'best' schools. That may in part be because these schools have had minimal experience of dealing with really awful events – events causing multiple pupil casualties, for example – or of seemingly minor incidents with awful consequences, so that when they do happen they really challenge the normal operating systems of the school.

The truth is, no school and no school leader is immune to bad things happening to them, and reputations and careers can plummet with remarkable rapidity. If you're a school leader or similar, then it probably won't happen to you, but it's better to be safe than sorry. After all, one in five teachers is falsely accused of something by a pupil, and one in seven by the family of a pupil. Even if an accusation proves entirely false and the inevitable investigation clears the teacher completely, the process s/he goes through can be extremely harrowing and the reputational damage hard to repair. As one very experienced and successful school leader under investigation at the time of writing has recently written (in an email):

'It's horrible being in a situation when you know you've done nothing wrong but can see how in the wrong hands you could be finished.'

The RMP is also about damage limitation. It's intended to prevent damaging and destabilising events becoming any more damaging and destabilising than they need to be. My experience is that the worst effects result not so much from the events themselves as from the way they are handled. They may not be handled ineptly, just not as wisely as they could have been. A number of heads have said to me words to the effect: *'If we knew then what we know now, we wouldn't have done or said the things we did'*.

Whist the RMP does not dissolve judgement-making, it is designed to minimise the need for on-the-spot judgements and actions, and to support and give confidence to your judgement-making.

The RMP can also be a vehicle for minimising Post Traumatic Stress Disorder for staff and sometimes the whole school community. When you experience a shock-to-the-system event, then you know that it's not just individuals who experience PTSD; it can be the whole organisation.

Is the RMP a stand-alone framework?

The RMP both complements other school protocols, policies and plans and also provides a wrap-around framework for them.

Virtually any school policy can be relevant. Some of the more obviously sensitive and provocative (in the literal sense of being potential triggers for school-harming events) include those for lettings, school trips, admissions, SEND, behaviour and, of course, safeguarding. But there are many others and a question worth addressing – especially by the school leadership team and the governing body – is the one in Panel 1.

Panel 1

Which of our many policies seem most likely to be triggers for challenging situations, especially when violated, or particularly relevant in terms of preventing and reacting to damaging events?

The policies/plans the RMP most obviously complements include:

- The Complaints Policy
- The Disciplinary Policy
- The Crisis Management Plan – including a Crisis Communication Plan (CMP)
- The Business Continuity Plan (BCP)

Your school will need and is legally required to have a Complaints Policy; like all others, it should take account of the latest DfE guidance and agreed best practice. The RMP should complement the Complaints Policy and tackle all other matters relevant to complaint responses that are not covered in the policy itself (we'll consider these later.).

Is the RMP a Crisis Management Plan (CMP)? The answer is both yes and no. It's a CMP in that it will help to avert crises or events escalating into them, but it's not a substitute for the CMP. The CMP is most necessary for any event that starts life as an obvious crisis – a fire, an explosion, a serious assault *etc.* The RMP comes into its own for an event that might not seem to be a crisis at the outset but then spirals into one – by, for example, media magnification or by the unremitting efforts of a tenacious and possibly malicious agitator. Many of the crises schools experience nowadays are of this kind: not obvious crises at the start. This is why a book like this is a necessary complement to already available guidance.

Much the same applies to the Business Continuity Plan (BCP). The RMP won't replace or reproduce what is in the BCP that kicks in when business as usual is not an option (when, for example, fire destroys part of the school building), but it will help to address difficult situations that arise as a result of what's happened. It will do for the reputation of the school and the confidence in those who lead it what the BCP should do for the functioning of the school: assure as much continuity as possible.

In many situations, the RMP will need to operate concurrently with one of the two operational plans. In other situations it will operate more consecutively – for example, when the implementation of the CMP or BCP gives rise to a serious but possibly vexatious allegation. The RMP will then 'take over' and guide the school in the responses it will make.

Ultimately, having an RMP represents an aspiration to be a school that is Ready for Anything. Of course it is only an aspiration, and a big one at that, but putting in place a comprehensive protocol that covers the prevention of, preparation for and responses to whatever the world might throw at the school is a key vehicle for achieving this aspiration. It demonstrates a proactive orientation to future functioning on the part of school leaders and other constituents of the school community (including the governing body). It needs to be accompanied by what we might best describe as a **turbulence-prepared culture** – one that will facilitate the transition, when required, from steady-state to shock-to-the-system. Having a RMP will be the agreed framework for ensuring that smooth (as possible) transition. Being turbulence-prepared (I shall soon describe this concept in more detail) will in turn help the school to be a resilient community.

What all this adds up to is a protocol that is much more than just a management plan or set of guidance notes – or, worse still, just another school document. The RMP is at best an expression of the will for **destiny determination** and the central tool for achieving it. No school will ever be able fully to control its functioning and future; the world is too complex for that and there are too many factors the school cannot control. But having an RMP, and the culture that goes along with it, is probably the best way for a school to feel confident that it will handle as well as possible whatever 'comes up'. An RMP is safeguarding for the whole school community.

What is the RMP based on?

Background sources for the RMP include, unsurprisingly, crisis management and emergency planning. The Protocol also draws on

Human Resource practice, though I make no pretence at being an HR professional and, in any case, the HR worldview seems hard to square at times with the reality experienced by schools and school leaders nowadays. Assumptions about the rationality and reasonableness of people, and about how problems can be resolved by giving 'support', just don't seem to fit so many of the frankly surreal, outrageously unreasonable and cynically orchestrated situations that I have encountered. **Complexity Theory** and especially **Chaos Theory** seem to be the better frames of reference for trying to make sense of what is going on.

Chaos Theory, for example, makes much of the idea of sensitivity to initial conditions, more commonly known as The Butterfly Effect, and this is often highly relevant. When things 'blow up' in a school, the relationship between cause and effect can seem tenuous, mystifying or bizarre. The old proverb tells us that from little acorns mighty oaks do grow. That's a partially accurate way of describing what happens with shock-to-the-system incidents in schools, but the reality is often more like finding that there's a tree to deal with when what you started off with looked like a tomato seed. It's so often a case of the unpredictable trajectory. Seemingly similar triggering events can result in totally different trajectories. The majority may soon turn into brief sparks and damp squibs. But one can rocket away on a path that no one could have predicted. That's what I mean by the dynamics of disproportionality.

Complexity theory, at least as I understand it, has also influenced my thinking. What complexity thinking (or complexity science) suggests is that with a complex system like a school it's important not only to do the right things but also to do them at the right times. What tends to happen in the real world is that there is a lot of freedom in the system in normal/ good times but a lot of tightening up in times of crisis. Complexity theory suggests that the opposite should be the case. Organisations like schools should regulate more when things are going well and allow more autonomy when things go wrong.

How come? In good/normal times, some staff members might be inclined to cut corners, make errors, be sloppy, do minor things they shouldn't and not do things they should, and seemingly get away with it. But misused or abused autonomy can accumulate and lead to small irregularities (or perturbations) that increase the chances of something going wrong. Then, when they do, the default response is to be more controlling, whereas the better response would be to allow more freedom to find ways to adjust to the new situation and the school to self-organise its way out of the crisis. Much depends on the capacity within the school and the calibre of its leaders.

As you will see in the following chapters, I place a lot of emphasis upon getting things right and regulated in 'normal' times so as to limit the scope for the problems caused by people acting in unsanctioned ways. Although I also offer specific ideas for responding to shock-to-the-system developments, the thrust of my 'argument' is: **the best time for prescription is before you need to dig yourself out of a hole, not during it.**

My thinking for the RMP has also been shaped by various aspects of psychology, by NLP (Neuro-Linguistic Programming), by PTSD and the themes of recovery from trauma, post-traumatic growth and resilience-building. All this chimes with the thinking in Nassim Nicholas Taleb's book *Antifragile: Things That Gain From Disorder* (2012). I hadn't read *Antifragile* when I designed the RMP, but Taleb's thinking involves ideas that are central to it:

- People underestimate how much randomness there is in the world.
- Many of the most important events are unpredictable.
- We can protect ourselves from such events, but also go much further than this by becoming antifragile – essentially, being able to benefit from shocks that come from randomness, volatility, disorder and stressors.

Some familiarity with the areas above would be useful to have, as would some degree of experience of and expertise in the following:

- Damage Limitation
- Disruption Reduction
- Stress Mitigation
- State (or mood) Management
- Surveillance

- Media inter-facing
- The law and legal procedures (essential)

Needless to say, all school leaders will have experience and, almost certainly, some expertise in all these (over-lapping) areas.

First steps

OK. So let's begin with the RMP proper. I'm suggesting that every school starts with two pre-response commitments designed to enhance its capacity for coping with turbulence. These will serve the school well even if it never has to respond to anything that is seriously destabilising.

Commitment One: We will put in place a programme for building the resilience of staff as well as pupils.

Developing an RMP and involving staff in it will in itself contribute to this programme. But the SLT or the whole staff would do well to address themselves to the following question:

What could we as a school do to ensure that our staff members are resilient enough to cope with unexpected challenges as well as known ones?

One obvious if indirect way of helping to meet this need is to encourage staff to focus upon developing the resilience and emotional well-being of pupils, as indeed most schools are currently doing, since this is bound to have a positive backwash effect on the staff involved. As the old adage goes: the best way to learn is to teach.

Commitment Two: We will put in place two plans, one to try to prevent any school-harming incidents ever occurring and one to prepare us for the possibility that they might.

The following chapter details some critical considerations for fulfilling the first of these commitments: preventing 'bad' things happening in the first place.

Chapter Two: Prevention Management Plan

This plan is designed to reduce the need to have any recourse to the response management plan. It's a plan to avoid the kinds of events that trigger the need for a response.

Step 1: Moments of truth

For reputation management and the retention of goodwill from within the school community, the SLT undertakes to identify **moments of truth** – those key to creating favourable or unfavourable perceptions of the school.

Moments of truth are those experiences that lead us to make up our minds about an organisation such as a school. A single moment can lead to a global judgement – unfair and inaccurate, perhaps, but that's what people tend to do.

We'd doubtless like to think that we make up our minds about an organisation through a rational, comprehensive assessment that takes account of all we know about it. In other words, our judgement is based on a wide range of evidence. But often our minds are made up on the basis of a particular experience that is meaningful to us. It works as kind of synecdoche: the part stands for the whole, and we assume that what is true of the part is true of the whole. If one member of the office staff greets a visitor badly on one occasion, then that visitor may leap to the conclusion that all staff members are unpleasant to visitors.

It's this tendency to extrapolate from the particular to the general that you are trying to tackle when you identify moments of truth, especially when a number of people are experiencing very similar moments. They can work in the school's favour (the Halo Effect) but very often they work in the opposite direction (the Horns Effect) when we project negative perceptions of one bit onto the whole.

Examples of moments of truth might include:

- How visitors are greeted and received (including when they phone the school).
- Impediments to contacting the school in an emergency (*eg* a continuous answer-phone).
- How a complaint is perceived to be dealt with (for example, seriously or dismissively).
- How mid-day meals supervisors deal with pupil incidents.
- Litter around the school.

How do you identify moments of truth? Sometimes people provide them unsolicited – as when a visitor emails with a complaint about how they were treated or about some aspect of the school – its decor, for instance. It's easy to dismiss them, but if they are not isolated and aberrant, then they need to be taken seriously. They can also be picked up through surveys and, more informally, by listening to staff and asking them to disclose moments of truth perceptions that they know about.

It's very important to press upon staff the **power of the single encounter**. A bad experience leading to an unfavourable view of the school can have the power of a **one-time learning experience**: once learned, never forgotten. It's the power of a traumatic experience or the kind that leads to a lifetime phobia. (No one ever forgets if they are scared of mice or spiders, once they've learned that they are!) The school wants as few moments of (negative) truth as possible, so trying to do things 'right' every time (a big ask) is important. A school with a parent who feels 'disrespected', and who translates this experience into the school could be a permanent thorn in the school's side.

Through the leadership team, the staff need to be told about the most common and critical moments of truth and urged to avoid creating them – ever.

Step 2: Grasp nettles

This is similar to tackling moments of truth, except that nettles aren't about isolated moments but rather about more chronic sources of disgruntlement and vulnerability. Grasping nettles is perhaps the most obvious and critical preventative strategy.

Schools, and particularly their senior leaders, tend to know what their nettles are, but sometimes don't have the courage or nous to grasp them. Obviously there is some pain involved; that's why they are called nettles not daffodils. But not grasping them is inviting trouble – almost literally. Nettles differ from school to school, but common ones include staff members whose performance or conduct is a long way from what it should be, dysfunctional staff teams, maverick governors, parents who spread rumours or rancour, bullying incidents that are never investigated or dealt with satisfactorily, health and safety hazards, on-going communication and relationship issues and, of course, a whole panoply of possible teaching, learning and curricular issues.

Grasping nettles means taking swift, often robust and effective action to tackle problems or situations with the potential to create them – often big time. It means not turning blind eyes or kicking cans down the road (to change the metaphor but make the same point). Ultimately it means, if you are in a position of leadership, doing what you are paid to do and avoiding future problems by doing so.

What stops school leaders grasping nettles?

Often what stops them is an unwillingness to experience short-term discomfort for much bigger long-term gains. This is a serious error of judgement. Nettles are problems that persist unless tackled. They can also normalise, which can be just as bad. If some people get away with doing what they shouldn't, then others may follow suit, because it just seems normal practice, just 'what we do around here'. And nettles of one kind can beget more nettles and nettles of different kinds because they all thrive in the same nettle-accepting culture. Not good.

What school leaders need to say to themselves by way of encouragement to take prompt, robust action is:

A day or two of discomfort for me now (taking tough action, putting up with staff dissatisfaction/resentment etc) will save my having to deal with problem situations for months or years to come.

Step 3: Pre-empting the problems that grasping nettles can bring

Nettle-grasping solves problems but it can also create them, particularly for the unwary. My experience is that headteachers and other senior staff members need to take one piece of pre-emptive action above all others: **ensuring that their governors (or trustees) understand that the nettles being grasped might squeal!**

If the head or other school leader is addressing performance or conduct issues, then he or she may not be popular with the staff concerned, and possibly with their mates on the staff. Staff may even accuse the head of bullying when what his/her action actually represents is strong and robust leadership – which in itself can be a shock-to-the-system event. (Virtually every headteacher in the land will know of fellow heads who have been forced out due to allegations of bullying.) If s/he is tackling a particular problematic parent, then some other parents might react badly, especially since they are unlikely to know the full picture. There may even be complaints against the headteacher. So s/he needs to prime her/his governing body with words to this effect:

I am addressing the poor performance of X department or X, Y and Z members of staff, so don't be surprised if you hear some grumbles. Just understand that these are actions that have to be taken for the good of the school, even if they create some short-term turbulence.

This may seem all very obvious, but I have known school leaders to lose the support of their governing body because it failed to appreciate this very point: that headteachers and others with leadership roles can be unpopular if they take the difficult actions they are paid to take. This includes actions against parents as well as staff or decisions that displease them.

There is one other point that I am tentative about making, partly because my 'evidence' is predominantly anecdotal and partly because it might seem like a generalised slight on younger staff members, which it is not. But it fits in here and I think it needs to be made.

In recent years I have encountered a number of schools where significant numbers of charges of bullying and insensitivity have been brought against 'older' and more senior staff members by their younger peers. In many instances the truth seems to be that senior staff members were simply giving directions to which some young staff took objection, possibly because of the nature of the directions themselves but mainly because giving directions seems to them too much like authoritarianism.

If this is indeed the case, then the head or other senior staff members need to help staff distinguish between being authoritarian (which goes down badly in an egalitarian age) and expressing legitimate authority – the kind of authority, for instance, that teachers (should) have in the classroom. Essentially, it's positional authority but blended with expert authority and possibly personal authority too. Of course, all authority and the directions which flow from its exercise need to expressed with respect and uphold the dignity of all concerned. If they aren't then there may indeed be grounds for complaint and the turbulence that this can bring.

Step 4: Minimise the potential for nettle growth in inherently volatile situations

Schools in certain situations are breeding grounds for nettles. This includes any situation where turbulence is factored in. Obvious examples include schools where staff turnover is high (for the wrong reasons), and schools that Ofsted has found seriously wanting and the parents agree. All such situations require strategies either for stabilisation or/and for improvement, compelling enough to secure the confidence of the whole school community.

Another very obvious breeding ground for nettles is any major change situation – a change in the status of the school, the arrival of a new-broom headteacher with clean-sweep ambitions – for example, a serious staffing re-structure or the implementation of a major internal change to which there is known or covert resistance. These are areas too big and too well-covered in other books on leadership and management to discuss in detail here. Besides, they are the kinds of big and transformational situations from which you might expect to experience very high levels of turbulence, whereas the emphasis in this book is largely on those seemingly minor and inconsequential triggers for the shockingly unexpected.

Even so, distilling change management wisdom into a few rule-of-thumb principles might be worthwhile:

- Don't ignore resistance; it only goes subterranean and then becomes much harder to detect and address.

- Help all involved to understand the motivations and reasons for proposed changes, even if they still disagree with them.

- Do all you can to prevent rancorous individuals from having a corrosive effect on others, on relationships, and on the culture; that might involve being tough with them rather than trying to appease. But put most energy into the 'neutral' or more open-minded majority rather into the negative minority; the latter are usually black-hole energy drainers.

- Ask staff (or parents, if they are the ones affected) if they would be 'willing to be comfortable being uncomfortable', at least for a while. You might be surprised at the response that this way of putting things can bring.

- Be very careful about the wholesale importation of (say) policies and arrangements that have worked elsewhere; they may not work in the new context.

- Spend time building faith and trust in you/your team before you require significant shifts in others or in their subscription to your change proposals.

- Don't over-load or overwhelm. Insist that your senior colleagues tell you if they think that this is what you are doing. Stressed and energy-drained staff are much more likely to do and say things, including to parents and in cyberspace, that, however unwittingly, feed the appetites of would-be trouble-makers.

- There are other situations where the potential for rampant nettle growth is much less obvious. One of these is the small school situation, particularly the small village school situation. Needless to say, many small primary schools are happily functioning places, and so I don't want to suggest that problems are inevitable in such schools. But my long involvement with them leads me to the view that new school leaders who embark on careers in village schools with the expectation that the school community will inevitably be happily cooperative and obliging are often in for a shock.

What 'innocent' school leaders may encounter but not bargain for is the level of parental power and possessiveness about 'their' school, a rather low regard for the *positional* authority and status of the head and other staff (even if they like them at a personal level) and their expectations about calling the shots. So new school leaders often start off on the wrong foot, allowing parents a great deal of access to them and to relate to them informally, almost as friends.

The typical trajectory is that the no-longer-new school leader comes to wish that s/he had started off on a different footing, had defined boundaries more clearly, had implemented routines for contact rather than allowing almost unfettered access, and had defined the staff-parent relationship more explicitly (and formally) and probably ensured that staff members understood their professional roles. (The latter often comes down to not gossiping and speaking indiscreetly with parents, understanding that their in-school role requires them to relate to parents as parents and not as friends, and to do nothing to undermine the authority of the headteacher and other staff members.)

Quite often, the leaders of small schools, feeling something close to being besieged by or at the beck and call of many of the parents, try to take action which leads to alienated turbulence. For example, they may put in place improvement measures that parents object to or restrict parents from coming into school whenever they fancy. The result is the growth of nettles that could have been avoided or minimised with effective proactive strategies, including establishing expectations clearly and strongly early on.

I want to stress again that I am not saying that parents try to rule the roost in all small schools. I am saying that senior staff coming to small schools need to come with accurate and realistic expectations of what they might find and not be lulled into thinking that things are necessarily going to be closer to a bed of roses than a field of nettles.

Much the same can apply to schools of all shapes and sizes. If new school leaders want to avoid some of the situations that trigger shocks to the system, then they need to recognise the potential for turbulence in situations where expectations and relationships are either poorly defined or not defined by those with legitimate leadership roles. The alternative is sleep-walking into nettles – a very painful experience.

Step 5: Minimise complaints and disgruntlement through policies that pre-empt them

Schools should know the areas that generate the most complaints and the sparks that could possibly start an inferno. The trouble comes when they are regarded as inevitable, so the school has constantly to respond to similar kinds of complaint or concern. Dampening a spark may not be enough to extinguish it or stop another flare up. This makes it a weak solution: weak because it doesn't get to the source of the problem and so will keep occurring.

One example, in primary schools in particular, is what happens at lunchtimes including, very often, the actions and reactions of mid-day meals supervisors (MMSs). In some schools, 80% of parental complaints come from this one source. This is not to denounce mid-day meals supervisors; they sometimes receive little training, inadequate supervision, too little integration into the general culture of the school and may also have esteem issues. If this is the case, strong solutions – ones that are persistently effective because they get to the root of the problem – are required so that familiar issues no longer occur or do so infrequently.

For the senior staff, the first step is simply to address the question: What might be the strong solution here? It won't be the same strong solution in every school, but in some it will be one which can be cast in the form of a policy. That is always a good move, because then it has status and strength, especially if it is supported by the governing body. For example, part of the solution to the lunchtime issues may be to implement a policy of only employing TAs who also do the MMS job at lunchtimes. It may take some time to implement this policy fully, but it can be stated as an intention. That should mean that supervisory staff operate at lunch times with the same protocols (*eg* in terms of behaviour management) that they use in the rest of the school day and benefit from the relationships they build with children all the time.

Another example involves fielding frequent complaints about children being upset. For many schools, this can be a major challenge and one that can prove incendiary. Of course, there may be good grounds for taking parental concerns very seriously – when a child is being bullied or treated harshly and unfairly by a member of staff, for example. But nowadays some parents seem not to understand that getting upset may often be just a normal response to something that happens, or that it betrays a failure to deal with a situation in an emotionally healthy way.

What could be the strong, pre-emptive solution here? One that I have suggested that has been successful is to introduce a Resilience Policy, and make the getting upset reaction a part of this. I've provided a bald, bold and uncompromising version of this in Panel 2 (overleaf). You will probably want to soften it, expand on the sentiments to help parents understand the thinking behind it, including the notion that parents can unwittingly disable their children by rescuing them (*ie* doing for them what they can and should try to do for themselves) and that getting upset can be a good and necessary thing to experience in order to better cope with setbacks and frustrations. You might also want to run a training session for parents on this, and perhaps also make it more explicit which kinds of upset will not be tolerated or dismissed in any way (such as bullying).

But once you have established a policy in which staff have conviction and parents (generally!) understand and hopefully accept, then you should have far fewer sparks to extinguish, and much less chance of any spark becoming a blazing inferno.

Strong solutions may not always go down well at first and some may take courage to implement, but the right solutions implemented in the right ways (robustly and confidently but with sensitivity and explanation) can substantially reduce the incidence of sparks and so the incidence of conflagrations.

Panel 2

Resilience Policy (extract)

We take safeguarding and our duty of care to children very seriously indeed. But we do not wrap our pupils in cotton wool or try to stop them ever getting upset. In the long run, doing this does no good whatsoever. If they are never 'allowed' to get upset, then they will never learn how to cope with the things that might make them upset, such as setbacks and frustrations.

Our position is that mollycoddling children and fighting their battles for them is disabling. Our intention is to enable them to be more resilient so that if they do get upset they can 'get over it' more effectively.

We are sure that you also want your child to be resilient, and that you understand that getting upset is both normal and sometimes necessary – even though it can be hard to see your child upset.

Be assured that if your child is upset (or worse) because of a totally unacceptable cause – such as bullying – then we shall deal with it robustly.

Step 6: Ensure that your eye is on the 'main ball'

This step applies only to school leaders (and other staff) with responsibilities for or in more than one school, or those who have a lot of engagement with schools or matters beyond their own school. Nowadays, particularly within a world of multi-academy trusts and other collaborative arrangements, many staff do.

Some of the school-destabilising situations I have seen have occurred in part because the headteacher (or other senior staff member) had allowed too much of his/her attention to go to schools other than his/her 'home' school. For one thing, doing this can mean not so easily detecting the nettles that need to be grasped or the moments of truth that make the school vulnerable.

This applies much more nowadays than it did even a few years ago with the rise in the number of 'leading' headteachers, executive headteachers, academy trusts and other familiar arrangements.

When school leaders have their attention split between different schools, then it can result in the situation I describe as gradually crumbling mortar. Weaknesses can be exposed; things can slip and slide; minor matters magnify before they are picked up and dealt with.

This is not an inevitable situation. Indeed, some school leaders seem to be even better leaders for having (say) dual responsibilities. They can, for example, better understand their 'home' school by contrast with the other they have taken on. Sometimes they can feel more energised and motivated by the challenge and better use the resources of the two schools. But it is vital to be clear about priorities and primary allegiances and, especially, to address the following question:

If I take on responsibilities for other schools or the support of other school leaders, can I do so confident in the robustness of my own school's culture and operations and confident that performance won't slip?

Governing bodies and trustees also need to be confident that the school will not be destabilised if they sanction their incumbent headteacher to give time and attention elsewhere. The question for them is:

If our head (or other senior staff member) is involved in supporting other schools, can we be sure that this will not have an adverse effect on this school and will not leave us vulnerable?

One practical measure is for the headteacher to put in place a schedule of briefing meetings. Through these, s/he can be furnished with updates by senior colleagues and others, so that s/he is kept fully abreast of developments and concerns.

Step 7: Ensure confidence in your policies

Most of the school-/personnel-destabilising situations I have had dealings with have been policy-related in some way or another: for example, a policy not in place or a policy violated or not implemented.

Get the SLT (or some other group) to conduct a comprehensive policy audit to determine whether all school policies are (i) in place, (ii) legally compliant, and (iii) clear and comprehensive.

To test your policies, address these two questions:

- Will following our policies greatly reduce the probability of 'bad' events occurring?
- Will they enable the SLT to respond confidently to any 'bad' events that do occur?

Once you are confident that you have in place the right, up-to-date policies, take action to ensure that all staff (i) understand and (ii) are committed to the implementation of each policy.

Take understanding first. It is all too easy to assume that staff members are more familiar with school policies than they actually are. Devote time to making sure that they *really* are. This should be regular and on-going. It could mean dedicating regular staff meeting (or equivalent) slots to highlighting the key points of policies. You may wish to make aspects of certain policies crystal clear, especially if there have already been problems with them. More gimmicky perhaps, you could have quiz-type tests to make the job of policy familiarity more fun. But do not make light of knowing policies. Staff members need to appreciate that they have a professional responsibility for knowing what is in school policy documents, though you may wish to identify those they should prioritise.

Staff can't implement school policies they don't know about or understand, and it is with implementation that some of the thorniest problems occur. Now here is the message that all staff – indeed all members of the school community – need to get clearly and unequivocally:

Policies are NOT optional

I can scarcely count the number of shock-to-the-system developments that I have come across that stemmed directly from policy violations. As someone who used to lead on behaviour for one of the UK's largest local authorities, I frequently had to get involved in serious school problems triggered by staff members not following the school's behaviour policy. But problems for a school can result from almost any policy not being followed.

What's the problem here? It's sometimes staff members doing the wrong thing at a moment of high tension – for example, responding to a behaviour incident in entirely the wrong (not in the policy) kind of way. But often it's not that. Rather, it's a casual attitude towards implementation. My experience is that some staff members have the view (remarkable as it may seem) that they can pick and choose which bits of a policy they implement and which they don't. They may believe that a policy is just a set of guidelines or a menu or an Ofsted checklist. They may believe that, since they don't agree with aspects of a policy, they somehow have the right not to implement them.

This situation is in part a failure of leadership. Headteachers and other senior staff members have not made it emphatically clear enough that policies are not optional. They have not insisted that staff implement all policies to the letter, even those they may disagree with or have doubts about. Of course, there should be opportunities for teachers and others to express misgivings or suggest adjustments to policies; that goes without saying. But once a policy has been agreed and endorsed by the governing body, then it is the equivalent of school law. It needs to be respected and implemented by everyone. Violations make the school very vulnerable. Indeed, school policies form crucial parts of the school's immune system, and that system is compromised and weakened when it is breached or broken.

I have spent many sessions with school leaders who have tut-tutted at teachers who display a *laissez faire* approach to policy implementation, or even flout the policies deliberately. My response is that frustration or resignation is absolutely not the right response to such teachers. It is the duty of any senior member of staff – indeed, any line manager – to insist that maverick or flouting behaviour is completely unacceptable. So is a casual approach to policy implementation. It's the road to possible hell. That is why all staff members need to fully accept that the implementation of policies is not a matter for personal discretion. Policy implementation is NOT optional. It's not a choose-to; it's a have-to (see Panel 3 overleaf).

Panel 3

'No. You can't opt out of a school policy!'

I was running a training day for all the staff of a large primary school. At coffee time, one member of staff approached me. What I had said in the previous session had clearly resonated with him; he saw me as a kindred spirit in terms of what he termed an 'enlightened' approach to behaviour management. He told me that he came from a background of psychotherapy and that he objected to the school's policy towards the management of reception children. He felt that it was not emotionally intelligent and that pupils had too few opportunities to express themselves. I asked if he had made his views clear to the headteacher, the head of Early Years and other relevant staff members. He said he had, but they were happy with the school's approach and the policy which supported it. He said that he couldn't implement it with any degree of integrity.

The response he wanted from me, I'm sure, was to agree with his philosophy (which I did as it happened) and to endorse his strategy of continuing to act in accordance with it. That was not the response he got. I told him that he had no option but to implement school policy – continue to suggest changes, perhaps, but still to implement it. Actually, as I pointed out, he did have a second option: find another job in a school that had a policy he could work with.

What applies to policies applies to standards, codes of conduct and procedures. If the school has agreed such things and they are represented in official documentation, then they too are not optional, and non-compliance can lead to developments that are school-harming. In a world where the dynamics of disproportionality seem to operate, the violation need not even be something most people would consider serious. It's obvious that having a casual approach to implementing a child's health care plan or violating the 'not having inappropriate relationships with pupils' bit of a code of staff conduct could/should have very serious consequences, but using a non-standard form of address to a pupil or parent? This too can be one of those molehills that become mountains.

Much can be gained from establishing the non-negotiables within a school, usually best done with the active involvement of staff. My experience is that the list should not be too long, but that there should be an attitude of zero or close to zero tolerance for the violation of any item that is included. Doing this ensures consistency in regard to core and key matters and ensures that staff members are not, as are too many children nowadays, limit-deprived! They know what is required and exactly where they stand, and they know support from senior colleagues may not be forthcoming if they flout a non-negotiable and it leads to problems. Then they risk becoming outlaws.

Again, school leaders must require universal subscription so that there are no points of vulnerability. It is vital also to ensure that supply staff and other non-establishment workers are fully aware of and committed to implementing the non-negotiables. Some of the most serious problems result from the ill-informed actions of unaware supply staff.

These actions are not about turning the staff into robots or clones of each other, and to complement the non-negotiables it makes sense to identify the areas where there is scope for negotiation by spelling out the latitudes of acceptable variation. But my advice is not to do this at the same time as establishing the non-negotiables. It can cause confusion. Let the 'must dos' become default settings and then identify the comparative 'choose tos' and acceptable differences of approach.

WARNING!

The ill-informed, sloppy enforcers and mavericks can all be very dangerous.

They make the school vulnerable.

If the school has an Achilles Heel, then they expose it.

Making a fuss

Another way of talking about non-negotiables is to talk about making a fuss. Something I'm very convinced about is that every school leader should get fussy about what s/he makes a fuss about but that s/he should definitely make a very big fuss about one or two things.

I experienced this as something close to a profound insight or epiphany in one of the first (large secondary) schools I taught in. I believe the headteacher was almost as new to the school as I was. All the staff thought he was a warm and avuncular kind of chap, and some regarded him as a push-over. Then one day at a staff meeting he said: '*If any member of staff lays a hand on any pupil he'll be out*'. This was at a time when corporal punishment was (just) still allowed and the school was heavily into it.

In one stroke, this seemingly easy-going and warm-hearted head had disclosed his hard centre. Staff perceptions changed in an instant. We all knew that about some matters this man was solid and uncompromising – that he had 'this far and no further' limits.

I was a very young teacher at the time but I knew there and then that every leader, every teacher and probably every parent had to have one or two matters about which they would truly make a fuss – and with full integrity, because it touched something that truly mattered to them.

To give one example, I was in the classroom of a very competent Year 5 teacher; his class clearly adored him and there was a tremendous working buzz. Then, suddenly, he turned from Dr Jekyll to Mr Hyde and let rip at a pupil. He then returned to normal mode. After the lesson, I asked him to explain his outburst. He told me that his one absolute rule was that no one treated his TA with any less respect than they did him. He called it his 'no diss' rule. Apparently, this pupil had just said something that the teacher thought disrespected the TA, so made his extreme disapproval very clear to both the boy concerned and the rest of the class. Like my early career headteacher, he made it very obvious that however good natured and allowing he might appear, he had a solid core that couldn't be messed with.

The effect of operating with a no-tolerance rule about one or two matters is that you come across as strong – strong by conviction. If parents as well as staff are aware that, however flexible a school leader is on many matters, there are a few things that s/he will absolutely not put up with, then that school leader is likely to both respected and generally not messed with. It is one of the most powerful ways of strengthening the school's immune system.

Violations: Can't or Won't?

I want to offer one note of caution – or wisdom – regarding the implementation of all the 'these things are not optional' matters.

Experienced and savvy school leaders know that for some staff regarding some matters, their failure to follow a policy is more a matter of *can't* than *won't*. Sometimes, for example, it's that they lack the confidence or the skill to take the action required, or that they are afraid that they might get it wrong if they do so. For example, I've encountered many teachers who feel that they lack the assertiveness skills to do some of the things spelled out in the school's behaviour policy or policy for interacting with parents. It also has to be said that sometimes staff members simply can't grasp what is required of them. They may not even know that they are failing to understand it. It's a cognitive issue more than anything else.

Wilful policy violations might lead those concerned down the formal disciplinary path, so it is very important to try to distinguish can't from won't situations before this is the route followed. Teachers are professionals and adults, so the onus should be on them to bring any challenges they might have to the attention of the relevant staff. If it's a skill deficit situation, or one for which they need some encouragement, confidence building or additional guidance, then make it clear that this is perfectly acceptable, and far better for them and the school than deviating from the 'have tos' by simply ignoring them.

It is harder to identify cases of not followed because not understood, but almost certainly there will be evidence of these, and it is up to other staff members to take action if they are aware of them. Line managers and the mentors of NQTs may be the obvious people to do this, but there are grounds for declaring the identification of unwitting policy violations a collective responsibility. After all, their consequences could affect the whole staff. So it makes sense to tell all staff not to be shy about pointing out policy infringements.

Step 8: Repeat a similar process for parents and governors

Ensure that parents are clear that the school has policies and that parents are expected to respect and follow them. Let them know, as you have the staff, that policies are non-negotiable (unless, of course, scope for negotiation or latitudes of acceptability are built into a policy). Again, this is something you need to come across as very serious about: courteous, of course, but insistent.

In reality, parents are unlikely to digest every relevant policy, so that drawing attention to really key bits of a policy on an as-and-when-necessary basis is a good thing to do. The same applies to standards and codes of conduct – those that apply to school-parent and parent-parent interactions, for example, or to standards of dress.

It is nearly always a good thing to make parents clear that the school's policies and standards have the backing of the governing body (which they should indeed have). It can make school leaders less likely to be targeted or to feel professionally isolated and vulnerable.

Step 9: Implement a 'Tell Us First' policy

Together with the Policies Are Not Optional policy, having and implementing a 'Tell Us First' policy with parents is probably the single most important action a school can take to prevent school-destabilising events occurring. In fact, for problem prevention, implementing the Tell Us First policy is *the* most vital of all pre-emptive strategies. It needs to be communicated to parents through all means possible and whenever an opportunity presents itself so that it becomes an ingrained default.

Again, it needs to be presented in a serious and insistent way rather than as a polite take-it-or-leave-it kind of request. Below is a version that reflects this, though each school will need to present it in the language and tone which best captures its 'house style'.

Tell Us First

If you have a concern about your child or are unhappy with something at the school, then please let us be the first to know. Nine out of ten times we will be able to sort a concern informally with you. Please do not turn to the Local Authority, the media, social media or any other organisation before we know about the matter and have had an opportunity to address it.

Together with the 'request' part of the policy:

- Make it clear that this policy has the full support of the governing body.
- Specify exactly who parents should come to with an issue if it is likely to be at all unclear.
- If class teachers are the first-line recipients, then make the reasoning for this clear and let it be known that the matter can/will be dealt with at a 'higher' level if necessary, but not initially.

There are two other requests (or polite injunctions!) that could and probably should be added to the Tell Us First one. They are:

Tell Us Soon (*ie* bring us concerns quickly rather than complaints late)

Leave it with us (to sort) … unless it is a matter for which you deem that parents should be taking full or most responsibility (see Panel 4).

Panel 4

'Is this our problem to sort?'

School leaders can sometimes get into trouble and aggravate situations by trying to sort other people's problems. It is worth asking:

Is this a matter that senior staff should involve themselves in?

Are we taking responsibility for something parents should be trying to sort?

Could we make things worse for ourselves by getting embroiled in matters essentially external to the business of the school?

(An example includes trying to mediate between feuding families. Some family feuds are inter-generational and hideously complicated.)

Should we have the courage and good sense to say:

'This is something for you to sort, not us.'

Or: *'Either sort your problems or leave them at the school gate; they have no place in school.'*

It might seem brutal to say 'Not our problem' but it may be the best approach for all concerned. If you refuse to 'rescue' certain parents – *ie* refuse to do for them what they should be trying to do for themselves – then this might make you unpopular for a while. But it might be the right and respectful thing to do and avoid the long-term problems of a hiding-to-nothing intervention.

Of course, there are many situations in which the best approach is for the school and parents to work together for a solution, but this is not always the smartest approach nor should it be the default one.

Why do schools need to operate 'Tell Us First and Quickly' policies?

Perhaps they always would have been wise to do so, but my experience is that it's essential now because many people seem to have a troublingly low threshold for getting outraged and being ready, willing and able to spread their outrage, especially through social media. What might have started out as a simple grumble can escalate into something disturbingly bigger: magnified in the source of the grumble and amplified by those who react to it. And it is all too easy to turn one person's outrage into collective outrage, a kangaroo court or even something close to a lynch mob.

If your school has a social media policy, then Tell Us First and Quickly can obviously sit alongside or be a part of it. It's almost impossible to stop parents and governors 'taking' to social media, and if your school has an active social media presence, then this is something you might positively encourage all members of your school community to get involved in. (I'll return to this topic later.) But you can ask strongly that parents and others (including governors) do not do so until they have brought their issues to the relevant school staff; make clear the reasons for this and point out the possible consequences of not doing so. These might include the intolerance for defamatory material and threats of legal action that a use of social media policy will probably detail, but more obviously that genuine problems might be very much harder to sort out. Of course, it's also a matter of courteousness and fairness.

You will almost certainly need and want to operate a similar policy for staff, though you may want to couch it slightly differently – as a No Secrets or Tell Us The/Your Truth policy rather than a Tell Us First policy. Staff members need to be asked to exercise discretion and judgement about what they deem to be matters significant enough to pass on to relevant senior colleagues, but insist that the furtive spreading of discontent is not acceptable. They need to inform school leaders of matters they are unhappy about, and it's absolutely necessary for staff to know and feel that they can do so with impunity. They need to feel comfortable being uncomfortable (see Panel 5).

Panel 5

Disgruntlement is Dangerous

- If there are discontents or malcontents on the staff, then better you know about their gripes and possibly justified grievances. You cannot manage or address resentment you don't know about.

- If necessary, flush out disgruntlement. Do not allow toxic discontents to operate with impunity or for ill-feeling to go subterranean.

- Don't dismiss concerns or get ultra-defensive. If staff members tell you things you don't want to hear – that they feel bullied, for example – then acknowledge those concerns.

- If discontents can do damage when you are present in school, then they can do even more damage when you are not. They can agitate, stir up trouble, re-write history and even implant false memories, especially if you are elsewhere (*eg* working in another school) for significant periods of time. Very few will, but it takes only one.

One major source of disgruntlement is the resentment of staff or parents. Sometimes it is covert and undisclosed. School leaders do not always pick up on the resentment or they under-estimate it. For example, and following on from the point above, I've encountered undetected resentment in schools with 'absent' headteachers – something approaching insecure or indifferent attachment or abandonment anxiety.

It is not always possible to remove resentment because that is not within the gift of the leadership – for example, when there are pay restraints or when teacher assistants are resentful that their pay is so far behind that of the teachers they work with. It does, however, need to be acknowledged and addressed as much as possible. Resentment that goes subterranean nearly always reduces discretionary effort and collective resilience – both vital assets to have in shock-to-the-system situations.

Policies: more is not necessarily better

I've made it clear that the policies need to be adhered to and that situations can turn very nasty when they are not. This does not mean that a school is necessarily less vulnerable if its policies are very detailed and full of prescriptions and proscriptions. Neither does it necessarily mean that a school is less vulnerable for having more rather than fewer policies.

Schools have to be careful not to be (too) fear-driven, and having policies to cover every possible eventuality is likely to be an indicator of being just this. There's a big difference between trying to prevent outlandish developments and living in constant fear of them. My experience tells me that a policy set up to deal with the extreme exception, as opposed to the norm, is rarely a good one.

Also, the more schools regulate, the more there is to push against and less the scope for using reason and common sense. Regulation – which is what policies and rules represent – can heighten the possibility of tension and conflict because there is much less wriggle room for all parties concerned. There are several advantages to not having everything pinned down firmly, one being that the school's hands aren't so tied – that is, it is not obliged into taking a particular course of action. Another is that relationships with parents are less formalised and potentially less antagonistic.

The same applies to notions of standards. To take an increasingly common real-life example, if your school has a dress or presentation code forbidding the display of tattoos, what do you do about a staff member you've appointed who has an undisclosed tattoo but was not aware at the time of appointment that this was an issue? What do you do about potentially great staff appointments that can't go ahead with the 'no tattoos' policy in place?

My suggestion is that schools discuss these considerations and come to some conclusion about them based upon their experience of policies in practice.

Perhaps the most fundamental policy a school requires is a policy about policies! That is a serious suggestion, and it might include some of the points I've just made as key principles.

Step 10: Consider whether the school should raise the 'effort threshold' for grumbling

One possible and perverse effect of insisting that parents bring their issues to you first and foremost is that they could come thick and fast. Moreover, some of the matters raised might be inconsequential or ones that will dissolve of their own accord. The question is: *Do you want to do anything to disincentivise parents from bringing you matters of these sorts – ones they really don't need to?*

I'm certain that different schools will come to different conclusions, depending in part on their current experiences and perhaps on the kind of relationships they have or want with parents.

Panel 6 presents some of the things to think about.

Panel 6

Considerations

Con: Better to be inundated with trivial concerns and grumbles than for just one undisclosed and smouldering gripe to escalate into a situation that finally rocks the school.

Pro: It can be useful to make raising matters slightly more effortful so that trivial and opportunistic ones never materialise. That means applying the **friction of effort** principle. For example:

Requiring parents to 'go through' reception staff who use their judgement to filter out trivial concerns; having set times for teachers to be available to parents; requiring appointments to see senior staff members; making sure that encounters are satisfactory but not emotionally rewarding or ego boosting; requiring letters rather than emails.

Step 11: Have a 'no ego displays' policy for staff and parents

The mechanism by which many minor crises in schools (and elsewhere) become major dramas is the **ego display**: the act of giving in to the ego's desire for expression and recognition. In some schools it happens a lot; in others, much less frequently and less obviously. Ultimately, its frequency and impact depends upon the ethos and values of the school and, in particular, whether all those who work at the school fully subscribe to and actively live the principle that 'we are here for the children'. Virtually all schools and all school staff would claim that they do. In reality, some people might be there more to meet their own ego needs than they'd like to admit or acknowledge.

Ego displays take several forms, but usually involve making a big enough fuss about an incident or a situation to feed the hunger for recognition. It might be an expression of self-importance: in effect, *'What a hero I am! Just look at me handling this situation!'* It might be more about self-pity: *'What a martyr I am to work one to one with this particular child!'*. Actually, they are both sides of the same ego coin.

If necessary, school leaders need to help the members of staff given to ego displays to fully understand what 'being here for the children, not for us' means in practice. And if necessary they need to insist that staff do not seek to feed their personal psycho-emotional hungers in ways which are not aligned to the business of the school. What school leaders can also do is feed recognition hungers in entirely legitimate ways by, for example, giving staff positive feedback, especially for the (low-key) ways in which they successfully handle difficult situations and challenging pupils and parents. This reduces the temptation to seek recognition in ways that are less professional and might cause avoidable problems.

In terms of avoiding 'bad things', the problem with ego displays is that they ramp up both the temperature and the profile of potentially volatile or actually critical situations. A critical incident that could have been dealt with quietly and calmly can escalate into something altogether more dramatic and consequential. For example, a fight that could have been broken up in a low-key way instead becomes more about the over-the-top interventions of the staff member concerned. It becomes a dramatic incident that gets talked about (and possibly magnified) with the risk that it begets further critical and destabilising outcomes.

One of the technologies sometimes involved in the breaking up of fights and other pupil-management situations is the use of walkie-talkies (or their equivalent). Whilst walkie-talkies can play an important part in staff communication and incident management, especially in larger schools, using them can also allow ego-related psychological hungers to get over-fed. Used in a discreet and low-key way they have obvious value; but in the hands of teachers rushing around and talking flamboyantly into them, resembling soldiers on military exercises, I have sometimes thought they can better serve the stimulation, power and recognition needs of those involved than they can the management needs of the school.

If this kind of thing becomes almost routine in a school, and it can in schools which are as much about the convenience of the staff as about serving the pupils, then conditions are ripe for all kinds of avoidable situations to blow up.

The additional problem is that if staff members turn crises (or even insignificant events) into dramas, then this encourages and legitimises pupils and parents to do likewise. In more extreme cases, schools can become unstable powder kegs where explosions are just waiting to happen.

So school leaders must make it very clear to staff and everyone else within the school community:

Don't turn crises – or any other situations – into ego display dramas.

Step 12: Make in-school surveillance a priority for identifying potential crises

My experience is that vigilant staff members make a school less vulnerable. School leaders need their staff members to be alert to issues while they are still nascent and only potentially problematic. This means no one on the staffing establishment ignoring anything with the potential to amplify or modulate into something more critical. It means enlisting staff members as the eyes and ears of the school – the school's immune system. No blind eyes. No brushing under carpets.

If staff pick up a bubbling issue – for example, by talking to or over-hearing conversations between parents or between pupils, or by observing pupils – then it might be able to be nipped in the bud. Some issues may take staff by surprise, but some can be anticipated. For these, the most effective approach involves: (i) identifying the 'look fors' and 'listen fors' – the indicators of the issue; (ii) asking staff to look and listen for these (which may also involve relevant training); and (iii) taking robust and effective action to address the problem, ideally at the deepest possible level (*ie* at source).

The mantra or formula for this could be:

Anticipate – Address – Avoid

A highly relevant example is mental health issues among young people. No school ever wants to deal with something as alarming as an attempted suicide on its premises. Needless to say, this does not mean that a school is directly to blame for the desperate acts of pupils, but the consequences for the school can still be traumatic. A higher-level awareness of its duty of care responsibilities and greater sensory acuity with regard to the look fors of poor mental health are key preventative measures for schools to take.

A question frequently to ask of staff is:

Are you picking up any early-warning signs of scary possibilities further down the line?

Schools in the independent sector with boarders are probably among the most sensitive to the potentially horrendous outcomes of not being vigilant enough to pick up the early signs of pupils with tendencies to self-harm – or worse. That is why many are investing heavily in on-site psychologists, counsellors and Directors of Well-being.

The general injunction here is: 'Notice More'.

Teachers and support staff are busy people and sometimes, very understandably, wrapped up in their own preoccupations and matters of the moment. Unfortunately, this can mean that they simply don't have the sensory acuity to pick up on things that really need to be picked up on. Busy-ness is always separating and isolating – and potentially dangerous. It requires sensitive handling, but staff need to be made aware that there is a need for peripheral vision as well as foveal focus, that their duty of care for pupils (and each other) requires a degree of othercentredness, and that not noticing critical 'look fors' could have serious consequences. In practice, this might require a combination of training (in, say, helping to better manage the psycho-emotional states of pupils and helping pupils to better manage their own states, close observation and the priorities for attention) and an encouragement to practise other-focused as opposed to self-focused modes of being.

Step 13: Make robust responses, including 'identify and confront'

Most schools benefit by presenting as both strong and caring – towards parents and, from those in leadership positions within the school, towards other staff members. It is a contestable generalisation, but my perception is that many schools nowadays, particularly primary schools, tend to be a lot more caring than they are strong. Many I've worked with say as much. It's important for schools to be strong **and** caring, not just one or the other.

A strong and confident school is not over-obliging, even for the best of reasons (*eg* securing the cooperation of parents). It doesn't give in to unreasonable parental demands, or seek to please and appease when it knows it's not the right thing to do. Schools and especially their leaders need to show that they are caring, responsive and helpful, but they need also to show that they are strong and confident.

One way they do this is through robust responses, including to those who seek to be unreasonably demanding or to seek to cower, intimidate or disturb. It's a form of tough love, and my experience is that schools that get a reputation for tough love experience fewer problems than those that are too ready to please and appease.

Robust responses take many forms: *'that* (your demand or request) *is not something we can do'; 'this* (your action) *is not acceptable'; 'our rule is, no one steps across the threshold of the school until they've stopped shouting'.*

One robust response, where a leadership team can show its collective strength, takes the form of identifying, exposing and confronting an individual who has tried to operate below the radar. It might be someone spreading malicious rumours or agitating covertly or trying to destabilise a situation or pretending they are happy with the action the school has taken about something but are expressing the opposite view behind the scenes. Letting the individual (or group) know that you are on to them and prepared to call them out and challenge them openly lays down a marker. It can deter others from acting similarly.

When the leaders of a school are strong but caring, then staff, parents and others know where they stand. It can also make them feel more secure. When the leadership team is the corporate equivalent of a competent carer, then staff and parents tend to trust that it will handle whatever 'comes up'. There are also likely to be fewer bad-intention individuals willing to 'try it on'.

Step 14: Consider taking personal protective action

School leaders can feel a lot more vulnerable than most people would imagine. Like the managers of football teams, they can feel like the fall guys for perceived performance failures at their schools – and with good reason, not through unwarranted paranoia.

So one question all school leaders should address is: *What am I doing to protect myself from professionally harmful developments?*

There are various measures a headteacher or other senior staff member can take, but one of the most important is a commitment to maintain and log a relentless focus upon what I call **causative action**.

This simply means documenting (and if necessary at a later date, demonstrating) the action that s/he has taken to address an issue that required addressing. It's 'causative action' because it is the action that the leader is taking to cause improvements, solutions and impact. It demonstrates that the leader is not a passive bystander, does not see himself/herself as a victim of circumstances or at the 'effect' of someone else's action, but someone who can act proactively and with efficacy. It's an accountability tool.

At its simplest, the recording of causative action can take the form:

'I took action X to address issue Y which had impact Z.'

Causative action is especially vital with regard to the following:

- Closing gaps – especially performance gaps (eg between one group of pupils and another)
- The critical few factors responsible for the schools performance highs and lows, including the 20% or so of actions that might have yielded 80% of returns in investment
- Acting on the advice of experts – for example, regarding personnel matters and specialist provision for individual pupils

Taking causative action doesn't necessarily mean that a school leader can demonstrate nothing but successful actions. But taking those actions and logging them is a hugely sensible measure for personal and professional protection.

It complements the process of ensuring distributive leadership in practice, so that the causative actions of the school leader are critical but neither sufficient nor determining for most school successes and failures. If all staff members take the actions they are supposed to take, then accurate attribution should be possible, and it will be illogical to hold the headteacher fully responsible for something that goes seriously wrong. What the headteacher has to do is cause all staff members to fully understand what is down to them to cause and, ideally, to model causative agency (as opposed to acting like a passive victim or blaming others).

Step 15: Log religiously

Schools vary a great deal in terms of their recording practices. In one local authority in London, 70% of incident and accident recording was done by just three schools in the last school year. Perhaps those schools were too fear-driven and/or undiscriminating in what they logged, but maybe they were wise enough to realise that they could never be certain what might come back to bite them.

Arduous as it may be, schools are less vulnerable if they log every incident and exchange with even the slightest possibility of becoming an issue at some later point in time. This includes the details of what happened, but above all the actions taken and the words spoken. My experience is that recoding should be as close to verbatim as possible.

Get down the exact words used rather than a summary or paraphrase of them. (Short-hand might seem an anachronistic skill, but my personal view is that every school would benefit from having at least one staff member capable of taking short-hand in critical meetings. Not everyone is comfortable with audio recordings, and word-for-word recording is much more effective and protective than paraphrasing and capturing the gist of what is said.)

One example of the better safe than sorry approach is to log acceptance and satisfaction. If, say, parents have sought an explanation or solution for something, and you have provided them with one which they say they find acceptable, then get them formally to acknowledge this. Then, if they change their mind later or do anything to express dissatisfaction (through social media, for example), you have the evidence that they were satisfied when they met with you.

Let me give two actual examples of this. The parents of a primary school boy complained to the school when their son came home with a chipped tooth. After meeting with the head and deputy, they said that they accepted that this was an accident and that they were satisfied with the school's handling of the incident. Subsequently, another parent suggested that they could make an insurance claim, and so they tried (unsuccessfully) to re-write history by blaming the incident on the school's negligence.

The headteacher of a school thought she had resolved a parent's complaint to the latter's satisfaction. The deputy then discovered that the parent had taken to social media to express her dissatisfaction – and much worse. The head called the parent in and asked if the parent was still satisfied with the solution. When the parent said she was, the headteacher presented her with a hard copy of what she had posted on social media. There was a lot of squirming in that office!

Step 16: Do your job as well as you can

This is bordering on stating both the bleeding obvious and the mildly patronising, but every school leader needs to do his/her job as effectively and ethically as possible. For all-round well-being, I would add as efficiently/economically (so that the job is done conscientiously but with no more time and effort than necessary) and ecologically (so that there is minimal collateral damage to all within the school community) as possible. For example, it's not good enough to prevent problems coming from adults outside the school if it's at the expense of the energies and good will of the adults within it.

Non-Attractor Schools and Non-Attractor Headteachers

Before we turn our attention to preparing for the possibility of shock-to-the-system events, I want to briefly consider the difficult question of whether it's likely that some schools and some school leaders 'attract' fewer such events than others.

To be honest, I don't have definitive or research-based evidence to go on. All I have are my own experiences and perceptions. They are based on dealings with many hundreds of schools and headteachers – but still subjective.

What I am absolutely certain about is that any school and any headteacher can find themselves in awful situations, and that includes superb schools and superb school leaders. Bad luck and circumstances play a part. One 'bad apple' on a staffing establishment, on a governing body or within a parent community can play an instrumental part. And so, of course, can action to prevent, prepare for and respond wisely to destabilising events, hence this book.

What I present below are my tentative conclusions based on my experiences. They have no more status than that, but I do believe they have some degree of validity otherwise I wouldn't be proffering them.

I am using the term 'Relative Non-Attractor' for a school that tends to experience comparatively few if any shock-to-the-system events or events that develop into anything like them. I'm using the same term for school leaders who seem to experience few if any events that escalate into something serious. Clearly, there's a hint in the term I'm using of attracting or inviting situations with the potential to escalate. That's only a sense on my part, but it does behove every school leader to consider whether there is anything s/he is doing that might be contributing to the unwanted situations they are experiencing. (It's the equivalent of teachers or TAs asking themselves whether they might be triggers for certain unwanted pupil behaviours.) It comes back again to operating from cause rather than from effect.

Here, for what they may be worth, are my perceptions:

Relative Non-Attractor Schools

- Parents are generally happy with the school and not particularly demanding.
- The school has no obvious Achilles Heel (*eg* no very 'weak' teacher).
- Often, the school is happy being graded as 'Good'; so are the parents.
- The headteacher/senior staff are trusted to sort problems brought to them, but generally not that many problems are.
- Parents generally are neither 'pushy' nor 'needy'.
- The school community is free of the seriously disturbed or malicious.

Relative Non-Attractor Headteachers

- Neutral, balanced manner: neither over-friendly nor unapproachable.
- Courteous but business-like.
- Not rattled; can't obviously be wound-up or intimidated.
- Not over-obliging, but still cooperative and responsive.
- Differentiated responder. Like a GP with little time for 'time wasters' but plenty for 'genuine' cases.
- Perceived as competent and trusted to sort things.
- Tries to ensure s/he gives no grounds for his governing body to lose confidence in him/her or to seek suspension or dismissal.

Chapter Three: Preparation Management Plan

However scrupulously you try to prevent school-destabilising things happening, they may still happen, and so your job is to prepare as best you can for that eventuality. That means (i) doing whatever you can to reduce the magnitude and impact of unwanted events and developments, and (ii) preparing staff and governors/trustees to handle them as confidently and wisely as possible.

Step 1: Establishing a turbulence-prepared culture

This is less a step than a development or transformation process. There's a whole-school dimension to the plan, and that involves developing a culture that makes it as turbulence-prepared as it can be. Having this kind of culture facilitates any necessary shift from steady-state mode (the school as it normally operates) to shock-to-the-system (possibly even crisis) mode. The key principle to guide you is: **minimal necessary change**. The less the change required, the easier and less destabilising the shift from one mode of operation to the next.

What this means in practice is not making the school feel and act like a different school when something potentially destabilising happens. It means having agreed and practised Plan Bs for when Plan As are no longer effective. The important thing is that they should be consonant and consistent with the 'normal' culture; they need to come from the same cultural stable.

Model SLD schools

Some kinds of schools tend to be very good at this, especially SLD schools that cater for youngsters with complex and profound difficulties. They absolutely have to be. If you cater for pupils with, say, autism who have aggressive behaviour outbursts or children with life-limiting conditions, then you will have to move into damage-limitation or crisis mode frequently, so it's vital that you have agreed fall-back routines. If thinking about contingency arrangements at a classroom level is second nature, then it's not a big operational step to thinking about them at a whole school level.

Model A&E departments

Schools can also look to hospitals for models of managing turbulence. Emergency departments are especially well-versed in putting in place contingency arrangements so that they can move from normal mode to a different level of operation if they need to – for example, when they have to cope with a sudden surge of patients following a mass casualty incident. Staff will know that in crisis situations they may need to switch functions, work even more closely as a team, acknowledge that standards of care may need to be adjusted *etc.* Schools need to do more of this type of thinking so that they too are ready for mode switching if and when necessary.

What contingency routines would it be good for your school to consider agreeing, putting in place and, critically, practising?

To summarise: the less change you have to make to cope with a change of circumstances the better it is. This is one of the keys to being a turbulence-prepared school. While you need contingency arrangements, the more they harmonise with your normal arrangements, the better they work.

A good illustration of this is a particular kind of turbulence-preparedness – **bereavement-preparedness**. A school that has to deal with the sudden, unexpected death of one or more of its pupils or staff, especially as a result of traumatic circumstances (such as a stabbing attack or a fatal coach crash) will almost certainly be in a better position to respond effectively if it doesn't have to morph into something it normally isn't.

For example, if the teachers in a school tend to present day-to-day as warm and caring, then the transition will work much better than if they suddenly have to turn into the strangely caring beings they normally are not. In bereavement situations, pupils need to be supported, not spooked.

In a bereavement- or turbulence-prepared school, 90% of its effectiveness in responding to shocking events comes from its everyday culture and operations and only 10% from special arrangements that have to be put in place to cope with an extraordinary situation.

So the question the school needs to address is:

Are we being and doing every day the things that we will need to be and do even more of in a shock-to-the system situation?

Contemplating that question might lead to the recognition that the school needs some new cultural norms – things that go on every day that could better set it up for shock-to-the-system events. The following are key contenders, the first two having already been highlighted:

- Staff being more other-centred and less wrapped up with their personal concerns. As I have already indicated, busy-ness nearly always separates and isolates, so that there is often too little awareness of the needs and performance of others. In a crisis situation, this cannot be allowed to happen.

- Staff not being allowed to turn crises into dramas to meet their own ego needs – for, say, recognition or stimulation. It's important at all times for staff members to know that they are in school first and foremost to service the needs of pupils rather than to gratify their personal needs. Most adults in most schools do realise this, but in some schools adults are allowed to escalate and exploit critical incidents for their own ends – to appear heroes, martyrs or miracle workers, for example – when dealing with acts of pupil misbehaviour. In true crisis situations, these ego-led responses ramp up the turbulence and make emotionally challenging situations even more challenging. Making ego displays a no-no at all times is the thing to do.

- Thinking and working in close-knit teams, so that team working will be second nature when it becomes even more necessary in a crisis. Close-knit team-work is critical to managing major incidents in A&E and hospital trauma units. It's just as important in schools when they have to deal with traumatic incidents.

Two critical questions to address

In a crisis, will staff pull together rather than apart? (There should be supporting evidence for the judgement made.)

Do we have routines for exceptional events that will kick in when normal routines are suspended?

Fire drills and evacuation procedures are among the most obvious contingent routines that schools have and practise, but schools benefit from having others and possibly alternative versions of the ones they have. For example, schools in the USA that have been subject to shooting attacks have learned the importance of having several evacuation plans so that they can select the best one for the situation (given the location of the shooter). Contingency plans for the re-deployment of staff and to launch a surge response to a threat situation are among the others schools need to consider. More on surge responses later.

Step 2: Scope the threats

This follows on from the 'nettle-grasping' of the prevention plan. While nettles are the problematic issues the school currently has, threats include new, potential and unknown challenges as well as the ones it is currently aware of.

A vital process is that of scoping the threats, risks, vulnerabilities and liabilities that the school may face, and then calibrating them to get some idea of their likelihood, possible magnitude and impact. Obviously, the school's experience may mean that it already has some sense of where the biggest or most likely threats are going to come from. For example, I worked with a special school that identified residential trips, lettings and sex education as its areas of greatest vulnerability. Another school highlighted the work of its mid-day meals supervisors, a poor deal for one particular class and staff's reluctance to engage with parents as the areas from which it expected problems might come. A third (primary) school highlighted its high-level dependency upon just one member of its leadership team in dealing with serious and sensitive issues with parents. It recognised that more senior staff members needed to step up to the plate and develop the competence to do so confidently.

One fairly obvious point: do not rely on Ofsted inspection reports to identify your school's threats, risks and vulnerabilities.

Scoping is a task for a group that includes leadership team members and governors/trustees.

The key questions to address as a result of the scoping exercise are:

Are there specific areas we need to take action on or exercise particular caution over?

Are we aware of any Vulnerability Exploiters – for example, school or local community members who may hope to take advantage of any weakness or vulnerability we may have?

My experience has led me to identify the most toxic of cocktails:

School Vulnerability + Determined Trouble-Maker

This combination is the one that many school leaders have told me they have come to dread. In truth, 'determined trouble-maker' is the more palatable alternative to the term they actually tend to use. That term is 'nutter'. Needless to say, it's in no way meant as a pejorative term for people with mental health problems or even for those the school might consider a nuisance for the issues they frequently raise. Rather, it captures the experience of school leaders who have been subjected to a sometimes unremitting onslaught of one kind or another by an often unfathomable and menacing individual with their own grievance or agenda. This person may initially appear reasonable, someone who just wants a problem sorted. They don't stay this way. School leaders have often said to me that these individuals should come with a warning attached. The problem is they don't.

> **WARNING!**
>
> Determined trouble-makers don't come with 'Determined trouble-maker' scrawled across their forehead or t-shirt.

It hardly needs to be said that individuals who present in a highly challenging way can be doing so legitimately and reasonably, or from a non-vindictive passion – such as grief, frustration or understandable outrage.

Indeed, one of the potential threats to a school can be a headteacher or SLT member whose own behaviour is provocative, defensive or unreasonable in some other way. As every school leader should be both practising and making clear to his/her staff, self-awareness is a professional responsibility, as is a willingness to review his/her behaviour in difficult situations. The same could be said of governing bodies and boards of trustees. *'Have our actions/responses contributed to the behaviour of the person we are calling a trouble-maker?'* is an important question to address honestly.

In schools where leaders have the confidence and the good sense to say to their staff members *'tell me the truth'* (ie, 'tell me the truth as you see it about the quality of my judgements and actions'), the chances of those leaders creating unnecessary problems, or even unwittingly contributing to their own demise, are greatly reduced.

Step 3: Consider identifying an Intelligence Coordinator (IC)

Having good intelligence is vital for being prepared for shock-to-the-system developments. In any school community there is a great deal of intelligence of one kind or another (reliable information, news, 'fake news', rumours, gossip), but much of it will never find its way to the people or places where it can be considered, filtered, corroborated and some of it used for the good of the school – particularly to anticipate future developments.

Having a formally designated Intelligence Coordinator – someone who can serve as the hub for intelligence about issues that are brewing or threats down the line – can be extremely useful. In practice, given the possible seriousness and sensitivity of some of the intelligence, that person will probably be someone senior. Staff need to be told that this person should be their first port of call for any information they have that might be significant to the future well-being of the school.

Of course, intelligence coordination can be a function included in the job description of an existing senior member of staff.

There are, in addition, IT-based systems for the capture, management and interrogation of information that can assist in the identification of potential issues. CPOMS (Child Protection Online Management System) is one of the better known and most widely-used. Recording for CP and safeguarding purposes are the primary rationale, but the software allows for the logging of a range of other related matters, including behaviour, SEND and family-related issues. One major benefit is that it is easy for staff members to flag up something, and they don't even have to do this at school.

Step 4: Enlist staff support for surveillance and intelligence gathering

This step complements the previous one. For the good of the school, ask staff to keep an eye out and an ear to the ground for intelligence that might be relevant and consequential, and to take it to the IC or input it to the relevant data base.

Make it clear that their duty is to report, not to act unilaterally, except in matters within their orbits of direct responsibility – as class teachers, for example. Even then they should be encouraged to pass on any information that might benefit the work of the IC. They should not respond themselves on behalf of the school – for example, to something they have seen on social media. In practice, the road to school hell is paved with good intentions.

This can look as if the school is being turned into a mini GCHQ, or staff made paranoid, but my experience is that it is better than being caught unawares by something that could have been prepared for or even averted.

As an alternative to having a formally designated Intelligence Coordinator, or to supplement or complement that role, schedule regular and frequent briefing opportunities for staff to share anything they think might be relevant. The downside can be the time lag between identifying and reporting, but there are upsides. It becomes the focus for conscious attention, vigilance becomes an explicit activity and there are formally sanctioned opportunities to report concerns.

Step 5: Make it clear to staff that as a school leader there is something you never want to have to say to the governors, the press or any other person or body: 'I knew nothing about this.'

Obviously this only applies to events that were known about but not disclosed, and ones that were deemed to have the potential to harm the school. It reinforces the No Secrets (and Tell Us First) approach discussed in the previous chapter.

Some people say that they like surprises, but it's rarely true: they usually only like the surprises they like. This applies to school leaders too; most of their surprises should be good ones. They should cause it to happen that they are rarely surprised by a potential or actual school-damaging development. Forewarned is forearmed. That's the advantage of an early-warning system, of course.

Step 6: Ensure there are no in-school silos

Allowing any part of the school to operate semi-autonomously or to 'do its own thing' carries serious risks. If any part of the school – a department or year group, for example – is allowed to operate differently from the rest of the school, then its latitudes of acceptable autonomy need to be made very clear and explicit. For me, the understanding should be: any part of the school needs to see itself first and foremost as a part of the whole and to express the culture and values of the whole. It will normally need to abide by the rules and policies of the whole.

It is the responsibility of school leaders to ensure that there are no wilfully maverick operators, especially at a middle leadership level, heading up sections of the school, for example. And the dangers of operating with too much independence need to be spelled out. If necessary, staff members tempted to push the boundaries too far need to understand that they may sacrifice your full support if things turn nasty when they do so.

One way in which silos can develop unwittingly and without intent is through relative physical isolation; for example, when they occupy a peripheral place on the premises or are 'off site'. It's important for senior staff to assure themselves that they are not turning into semi-autonomous units by default. Staff in such settings should be encouraged/required/enabled to have frequent encounters with staff in the main body of the school. Relevant here is the following observation by Gillian Tett (2015):

'The longer the walk to the loos, the more likely the firm is to succeed.' [1]

But silos and semi-autonomous teams can evolve even when there is little physical separation involved. I've sensed their development in the pods of some new-build secondary schools and among groups of therapists in SLD schools. The process doesn't even need to be conscious or intentional, and there may be no attempt to form any kind of break-away unit. It just happens by virtue of a group of people working closely together and developing a culture with its own particular flavour. It needs watching out for and teams need to ensure they don't become sub-groups with their own separate culture. Of course, there are advantages in having tightly knit teams, but not if they operate by an aberrant set of rules and values. School leaders need to ensure their subscription to the schools policies and non-negotiables.

But there's also work to do at the level of mind-set. What potentially semi-detached groups need to understand is that they are not just part of the whole school but they are also the school in part. They need to have and operate with what might be called a **microcosmic mind-set**. That is, they need to see themselves as miniature versions of the school as a whole, so that their actions are as much as possible in the best interests of the school as a whole.

There is a corollary to avoiding silos in schools. If an issue does occur,

---

1 Tett, G. (2015) *The Silo Effect: The Peril of Expertise and the Promise of Breaking Down Barriers*, Simon & Schuster.

and it is specific to one part of the school, then seek if possible to confine it to that part of the school. You may need a containment strategy to seal it off and prevent creep or contamination. That might take the form of an assertion of accurate attribution – a statement that 'sets the record straight'. For example:

'We had an isolated issue in the Foundation Stage which has now been happily resolved.'

If a potentially school-destabilising event has affected one bit of the school, then at least the rest of the school can escape being tarred with the same brush.

Step 7: Consider identifying a Media Manager

Your school may already have at least one senior person who has been trained to interface with the media and is regarded as having the attributes and skills to do this successfully. This person may well be you. If you don't have an explicitly identified media manager/press officer, then you might benefit significantly from having one, especially if you are a school that no longer has automatic access to a local authority press department to which you can refer and, if you are lucky, get the support you need.

The Media Manager would normally be someone senior and might even be a governor or trustee member with the time, skills and experience to play the part. The Media Manager will be the school's principal spokesperson and PR representative, though the headteacher or chair of governors might also fulfil this role in serious situations.

The Media Manager could also be the Intelligence Coordinator, but the roles are complementary, so not necessarily so.

Obviously, the Media Manager will have a pivotal role to play if the school finds itself in a position where it will have to explain itself to the outside world. But arguably the even more important role is that of pre-emptive protection through continuous reputation management. With the support of others (*eg* office staff, media savvy parents and governors) the on-going responsibility of the Media Manager is to ensure that the reputation (good name) of the school is built, enhanced and maintained with all stakeholder groups, including those external to the school – other schools; media organisations; if it's an LA school, with the local council and its officers *etc.*

This will involve, for example, the provision of good news stories (obviously) and perhaps less obviously the cultivation of good relationships with journalists and influential others. (Journalist and media friends assure me that if they have easy access to 'good' news items about a school and positive relationships with named individuals, then they are less likely to dig around for 'bad' news when a situation breaks.)

The rationale is obvious: **build and manage a positive reputation for the school in normal times and this will reduce the negative impact in times of trouble and turbulence.**

Ongoing reputation-management is a crucial part of risk-reduction and harm-protection. It's a key strand in safeguarding for the school. It's about regularly boosting the school's immune system.

What all senior managers and governors need to ask themselves, not once but regularly, is:

Are we confident that we have established a supportive and protective relationship with at least the vast majority of parents?

One crucial reason to have a protective school community is that within it exists the social and peer pressure to de-potentiate any individual or small group who seems unfairly to 'have it in' for the school or the headteacher or other respected staff member (see Panel 7 overleaf).

Panel 7

'Stop it!'

For reasons that have never fully emerged, the father of a pupil at a highly regarded primary school began a campaign to vilify and intimidate the headteacher. The long-standing head was extremely popular with parents, but for some reason this particular parent set out to make life as unpleasant as possible for the head. The head recounted to me both his efforts to engage the parent (which all failed) and what he suffered at his hands, including having the parent stare daggers at him every day in the playground. I'd known the head for a long time, known him to be a strong and confident leader, but saw him reduced almost to tears at the treatment he was receiving from his tormentor.

The school was multicultural, and the parent concerned was from the largest of the ethnic groups. Since it was a supportive sub-community, I suggested that the head should ask some of its representatives to see whether they could 'have strong words', or something to that effect, with the malcontent. That's exactly what they did. They exerted the kind of social pressure that neither the governing body nor the local authority could bring to bear. In all honesty, no one enquired too deeply into the precise methods the parents and community leaders used, but they had the desired effect. The parent concerned no longer targeted the head or posed a threat to the well-being of the school.

There are, of course, laws to protect people from harassment and other forms of distressing and threatening behaviour, and schools should have recourse to them if necessary.

With a supportive school community behind them, the senior leaders and staff of a school can feel confident that the main body of parents will step in if they perceive a patently unfair and undeserved attack on the school. What they want to hear if necessary is:

'Hands off our school!'; 'Hands off our school leader(s)!'

Step 8: Agree or decide your school's organisational self-image

This is an extension of reputation management or, rather, a necessary precursor to it. A school needs to know how it wants to 'come across' before it consciously presents itself to the world. Otherwise, it could be presenting the 'wrong' or mixed kinds of images and messages.

The better a school knows itself, the easier it will be for others to know it.

This is about much more (or perhaps much less) than standard self-evaluation and data analysis. It's about the actual values it operates by (as opposed to those it declares – if the two don't match) and about the relationships it has with constituencies within the school community and beyond. If a school knows and is happy with how it is perceived, then it can express this through its 'house response style' or what other organisations might call their corporate presentation style. This style will be expressed in and through everything the school 'puts out', including its marketing literature, communications with parents, prospectus, policy documents, website, social media output and actions.

If there is clarity and consistency about this style, and confidence in it, then the school will know the response style in which it will respond in a shock-to-the-system situation. It may choose or need to make some tonal adjustments depending on the situation (for example, come across as a fraction more or a fraction less business-like) but the style will be essentially the same and consistent, so that the school still comes across as fundamentally the same school.

So a really important question for staff and governors to address is:

Do we have a response style that matches the kind of school we are and the kind of relationship we want with parents in particular?

In considering its organisational self-image and the house style that reflects this, a school would do well to capture its essence as pithily but powerfully as possible. Obviously this needs to be an accurate representation of its current state or, at least, a vision statement of what it is moving towards. It's all about emphasis and combinations.

For example, a school might see itself and want to come across as, first and foremost:

Business-like and professional; or

Familial and obliging; or

Strong and caring

Of course, these are crude pairings and there are all kinds of other fusions and possibilities, but at least they suggest the kind of thinking a school needs to do to decide what we might call its identity, its character or, to choose a different image, its organisational operating system.

The clearer and more secure a school is about this, the more confidently and better prepared it is to handle whatever comes up. A secure self-image enables a confident response.

Clarity about its relationship with parents is especially crucial. Does the school have/want/operate an arm's-length relationship or a much closer one? Would shifts in one direction or another increase the likelihood of destabilising developments?

One interesting typology of school-home relationships is that presented below, from an American book called *Beyond the bake sale: the essential guide to family-school partnerships* (Henderson, 2007).[2]

1. Fortress
2. Come-when-we-call
3. Open door
4. Partnership

Any school needs to be clear about and satisfied with the kind of partnership it has, and the above model might provide the starting point for staff or staff-governor/parent discussion. That relationship will make all the difference to how things fare when things threaten to go belly-up.

My own observation is that quantity of engagement is not the same thing and doesn't necessarily correlate with quality of engagement. So,

---

2 Henderson, A. T. (ed) *Beyond the bake sale: the essential guide to family-school partnerships*. The New Press.

for example, it might be wrong to assume that we, our school, is going to experience fewer problems if we encourage or allow parents unfettered access to staff – to give the message that we are nearly always available and accommodating.

Similarly, it might be wrong to assume that if we have a more arm's-length and a more gate-keeping relationship with parents, more potential problems are likely to occur. These are all-too-easy assumptions to make, and my experience makes me wary of making them. I've worked with schools that have experienced serious problems because or in spite of being ultra-accommodating to parents. I've also worked with schools that are generally happy to keep parents at the school gate, but deal effectively with issues if and when necessary, and have little experience of serious turbulence.

Step 9: Develop the communicative sensitivities of staff

Whatever the school's relationships with parents and others, staff members need to exercise a high level of discretion about what they say and how they say it. This has always been the case, but nowadays it is even more important given how willing some people are to pass on ('post') what they are told or hear, and given how easy it is to disseminate those words to innumerable others in the blink of an eye.

School leaders and Media Managers need to guide all staff to be careful, thoughtful and even guarded in what they say to each other, to parents and others so as not to risk damaging the reputation of the school or, more likely, being (deliberately?) misconstrued or triggering unwanted reactions, including allegations.

Put simply, it is up to school leaders to discourage staff from being seduced into too much familiarity with parents and others. 'Seduced' implies deliberate intent with motives, and senior staff must advise all staff to avoid falling into traps for the unwary – in particular, not feeding the appetites of those who thrive on vexatious misconstruction.

This can be especially challenging for younger and less experienced members of staff, and for almost all teachers in primary settings where contact with parents is likely to be close and frequent. But all staff in all schools need to be wary. Nowadays, of course, over-familiar exchanges, gossiping and incriminating revelations can occur online through social media sites, blogs and chat rooms as well through face-to-face encounters.

Like carelessly discarded matches, throwaway remarks can cause fires that prove hard to put out.

Even totally innocent remarks can be misconstrued, and the consequences can be serious (see Panel 8).

Also: don't feed the appetites of those who thrive on vexatious misconstruction.

The question senior leaders and governors need to address is:

Are all our staff members careful and savvy communicators?

What applies to staff members applies also to governors. They too must have a keen regard for what they say about the school to people outside the school and to parents.

Be aware also that parents (anybody) can record conversations on their mobile devices without your knowing. The fact that this should not happen and won't furnish legitimate evidence for allegations or other uses is not the point. It can happen and it can cause problems.

Panel 8

A teacher was having a pub lunch one weekend with her husband when she spotted and briefly acknowledged a parent who was eating and drinking with friends. On the following Monday the teacher encountered the parent and said to her in a friendly and, to her mind, totally innocent way, 'It looked as if you were having a good time in the pub on Sunday'. She was shocked a couple of days later to discover that the mother had taken to social media to complain about (i) being spied upon by the school, and (ii) being accused of being drunk and disorderly. The parent was not placated by the teacher's and school's reassurances that no such meanings were intended, and she persisted in making life difficult for the teacher concerned.

Step 10: Ensure role clarity for those with dual roles

My experience is that a lot of the problems related to loose talk occur because staff members or governors do not fully appreciate the constraints and obligations that their professional or formal role places on them. If they are parents (or local community members) as well as teachers and TAs and governors, then they need to separate what is acceptable to talk about in their in-school role from what is acceptable for them to talk about as parents. Conflating or confusing roles can get them and their school into deep water. In an age of social media, this is even more the case, and teachers need to be wary of contributing to networks (for example, being Facebook friends with parents) and online forums in ways that potentially conflict with their professional roles.

This is another area that school leaders need to explain and get very serious about, so that anyone who does, for example, reveal matters that are confidential or they know only by virtue of their in-school role, should be fully aware of the possible consequences of doing so. On most of the occasions when loose talk does create problems, it is just that: loose talk, with no intent to cause trouble. But schools cannot afford thoughtless disclosures, and just one of them to the 'wrong' person can cause almighty problems. Social media has made gatekeepers of us all.

Step 11: Create and practise scenarios

Many schools are likely to think that they have enough actual challenges to deal with as it is, let alone getting into the business of making up possible future ones. My experience is that doing just this is one of the best ways of preparing for the unexpected – expect it and consider the best response to it or, better still, what might have avoided it in the first place. Scenarios or simulations can be devised in-house or with external support.

This can be done at two levels. First, at the school leadership level. The leadership team (perhaps with governor or trustee participation) can consider possible or actual situations and then consider how those situations could and should have been prevented. The second level would involve professional development activities for middle leaders in the form of an assessment centre, where they would handle 'real world' simulations, have them assessed and then receive feedback on their performance.

One area that assessment and feedback would inevitably focus upon is judgement. It is remarkable how little training for school leaders is designed specifically to develop their judgement, and yet this is arguably the number one competence required for successfully handling the situations from which school-harming or self-harming consequences can issue. A well-designed assessment centre presenting potential school-destabilising scenarios to prepare for or respond to could both test the quality of an individual's (or the leadership team's) judgement and be the basis for improving it. Does this person/team: (i) show caution when it's required? (ii) prioritise effectively when necessary? and (iii) arrive at high quality judgements? These are some of the questions that need to be asked.

Step 12: Use or devise a tool for Impact Awareness

To both prepare for and respond to events systematically, one critical question to address is:

On whom and on what will this development impact?

To map where the impact is likely to be felt, and to ensure that no areas of negative impact are over-looked, a comprehensive mapping tool of some kind is almost indispensable. In the box below, I've offered one such mapping tool that I've devised and used, specifically with school events and organisations in mind. It has been inspired by a model created by integral philosopher Ken Wilber (opposite, from *A Brief History of Everything*, Second Edition, 2001).

Four Quadrant Impact Model	
INDIVIDUAL	
Increase in stress, anxiety and other disturbed states Poor mental focus Well-being deteriorates Health declines	Role fulfilment issues Time management problems Routines disrupted Negative impact on teaching Physical effects such as poor sleep
INTERNAL	**EXTERNAL**
School/team climate poorer Less sense of togetherness Sense of alienation Morale poorer Values shifting	School operations affected Harder to maintain time-tables and routines Slippages in improvement initiatives More staff/staffing issues More meetings required Greater external demands
COLLECTIVE	

This seeks to be a comprehensive model since it maps the impact of a shock-to-the-system event on both individuals (individual dimension) and the whole school (collective dimension) and for each of these areas both their internal impact and their external impact. The upper-left quadrant maps what can happen to the insides of individuals when they experience disturbing and distressing situations, especially if they are prolonged. The upper-right quadrant relates to changes in individual behaviour. The bottom-left quadrant is about the school culture and relationships and the bottom-right quadrant maps how systems and operations can be affected. Needless to say, the details I've provided in the model capture just some of the specific areas of possible impact.

Mapping impact can help to identify priorities, often shifting priorities, so that attention can be given to whichever areas are deemed to be most affected or most critical to the effective functioning of the school. In at least two of the schools I've worked with struggling to cope with seriously destabilising developments, the most obvious area of impact was on the leadership team, both as individuals (some more than others) and as a team. None of them was prepared by previous experience to deal with the situation that confronted them; they were all being pulled away from their regular roles and all were losing confidence in their own skill sets.

A protracted crisis can impact different staff members very differently and they can also seek to manage the impact on them very differently. The Four Quadrant model enables these differences to be mapped. It could profitably be used in tandem with a tool that identified the coping and support preferences of each key player. Knowing these enables colleagues to honour and work respectfully with these preferences, even if they differ significantly from their own. For example, one senior staff member might want emotional support from colleagues to cope with raised levels of stress whilst another might want more practical, hands-on help for coping with new or unfamiliar work tasks.

Step 13: Consider whether the school would or would not be better served by a full embrace of Facebook (or other social media platform)

This step might be irrelevant if you are in a school that already does a great deal of school 'business' through Facebook and encourages staff and parents to engage fully with it. If that is a step you have taken, then rolling back on it would be extremely difficult to do, even if it's something you might like to do.

My experience is that some schools swear by the benefits that Facebook engagement has brought them, and others (the majority) are wary of extending the level of engagement they have. I have no recommendation to offer, one way or the other, but Panel 9 lists some of the possible benefits and costs. For a largely one-sided view of things, the experience of one primary school, you might want to read 'Status update: Facebook is perfect for parental engagement', by Christina Zanelli Tyler, headteacher of West Cliff Primary School in Whitby (*TES*, 23rd September 2016).

Panel 9

Should we go for a full embrace of Facebook?

Possible gains

- More parental involvement
- More parental goodwill
- Knowing more about our pupils and families
- A more knitted-together school community
- Fewer complaints about us going unseen
- More opportunities to nip problems in the bud

Possible costs

- The time it takes to post and respond
- Having to be forever available
- Fulfilling (possibly unrealistic) expectations that we have created
- Knowing more than we can cope with or use
- The level of personal exposure
- Being regarded as a friend/familiar and its effects on relationships with parents

---

Step 14: Future-proofing relationships

When planning for the kinds of circumstantial changes a shock development can bring about, one really important area to think about and anticipate is that of relationships. My experience is that these can change more radically and disturbingly than those affected would ever have believed. I've seen relationships sour and for the bitterness to continue well after the development reached some kind of conclusion. I've known headteachers shocked at what others have revealed about themselves, overtly or simply by their actions. I've seen relationships strained to breaking point within leadership and other teams that would once have considered themselves tightly knit and highly robust. I've worked with headteachers desperately frustrated and impotent because they couldn't put records straight or have any significant communication with those they felt they needed to. And I have supported headteachers who felt alienated even from themselves.

I've also seen just how wonderfully and mutually supportive the members of a leadership team can be for each other.

There is no way of being certain of exactly how things will develop once a shock-to-the-system development occurs, but I do believe that action can be taken to future-proof them – at least, to some degree.

The image I use to capture one aspect of this is that of the draw-bridge. Putting in place pre-emptive arrangements to deal with possible future situations is like making sure there's a draw-bridge for when you are beyond the moat.

Relationship with self

Anticipating a possibly different relationship with your self is the first relationship to consider. Part of this involves psycho-emotional preparation for what might be substantial, even traumatic, challenges to your sense of self and self-regard. Building your personal resources and resilience while the circumstantial sun is shining is one thing to do.

Coaches and mentors can sometimes help here. One fundamental area to work on is self-awareness; you can't make changes to aspects of yourself that you don't recognise or you seek to deny. This in itself can both take and enhance your courage to confront difficult matters. Some of the headteachers I have worked with have discovered things about themselves that they'd wished they'd known about and faced long before trouble can along – their over-identification with their job, for example, or their over-strong approval driver.

Another strand of preparation is almost the opposite to the one above: it's reminding yourself that you are fundamentally the same person when events or others seem to suggest otherwise, and that you actually carry a lot of 'knowns' when you move into the unknown. For example, there will be knowns around what you have successfully dealt with in the past, and you will need to frequently remind yourself of these reference experiences. Doing so is ensuring that there's a draw-bridge to your own essential and continuing self.

The personal and self-relationship issues that I have come across include: identity issues (*'Who or what am I now that I'm no longer the highly regarded school leader?'* – especially problematic for those who have conflated their role with the whole of their being); not recognising the person they have become; dwindling status and diminished self-worth; shift to an insecure child ego state; assertiveness problems, presenting either more submissively or aggressively than they are accustomed to doing; and impaired self-trust, including a loss of confidence in making decisions. (One measure of how seriously affected someone has become is that they find it hard to make even trivial decisions – whether they want a coffee or not!)

Obviously, no one wants to spend endless hours imagining the worst case scenarios and how they might be impacted by them, but giving some time to the psycho-emotional rehearsal of possible future situations can make dealing with them in reality less strange and more effective.

When a school leader finds herself/himself in a situation they could never have imagined, then they quickly learn just how robust and resilient they really are. The intent in the 'good times' should be to build these personal resources so as to score as high as possible on what some psychologists call the Adversity Quotient (AQ) when things turn truly challenging.

One place to start might be Taleb's book *Antifragile* that I referred to in Chapter One. How good it would be to discover that you could not only withstand adversity but benefit from it. Similarly, some familiarity with the field of post-traumatic growth could also serve you well if you should ever experience traumatic events in a school context.

Relationships with others

This is all about taking pre-emptive action to try to secure relationship preservation and persistence in times of high stress and challenge. I've found that the very act of talking about keeping relationships going and keeping them recognisable, with partners and with close work colleagues, can be very helpful. Devote times to doing this when the going is good.

One common understanding that needs to be established through talking together is that relationships might alter if something extraordinary happens, and there is nothing wrong with this – indeed, relationship adjustments might even be healthy and necessary. For example, in one SLT I worked with, it was acknowledged that if there was a mighty blow up with a parent then the deputy might be the better person to take the lead since she (it was agreed) was better than the headteacher at keeping her cool in explosive situations. Within the same SLT it was anticipated that one of the other members would probably withdraw even more than usual, but that would be OK because she could work by herself on tasks the others might neglect or find too demanding or too detailed.

The other key to relationship persistence is simply a commitment by all concerned to do whatever is possible and allowable to maintain connection and relationships, however testing it might prove. (Of course, someone might invalidate that commitment if they are themselves the obviously guilty party.)

Relationship with governors

This is a crucial relationship for any headteacher, and several of the serious relationship fall-out issues that I have encountered in relation to school-destabilising developments have involved this one.

I am absolutely convinced that every governing body and every headteacher should talk to each other about the importance of aiming for relationship persistence, and the opportunities there might be for keeping the draw-bridge between them down should anything go seriously wrong.

Of course, under certain circumstances (such as when a headteacher is suspended) there may be a legal requirement to close off most of the normal official channels of communication. That does not preclude talking about relationship persistence and considering what commitments, if any, each party might make to maintain it.

Here is a question I have invited governing bodies to address:

Is there anything we can do to future-proof our relationship with the head or to ensure that things do not fall apart any more than they need to in the unlikely event of something 'going wrong'?

I've suggested to both headteachers and governing bodies that they might wish to explore the possibility of framing some kind of covenant. This would: (i) serve as a bridge in the case of a relationship hiatus; (ii) avoid the possibility of physical separation without an 'understanding'; and (iii) avoid the possibility of the headteacher feeling deserted or isolated if it doesn't have to be utterly that way.

To explore the content of a possible covenant, both the headteacher and the governing body could ask the questions to which they most want answers and assurance. Those that follow may not be the ones they may wish to put, but they do fairly reflect the areas of concern to some of the headteachers and governing bodies that I have worked with. I'm not proposing these as lists of questions to reel off. Rather, they serve as guidelines for the discussion.

Covenant framing: the Headteacher's perspective

Q. Can I be confident that no governor will act unilaterally?

Q. Can I be confident that individual governors will always act in ways that will not undermine me, even when I'm not in sight or/and others turn against me?

Q. In the event of 'maverick' individual governor actions, can I be assured that the governing body as a whole will have the courage to address this – no matter how uncomfortable?

Q. Can I be sure that individual governors will keep me informed of any perceived discontent that could affect relationships within the school?

Q. Can I be sure that you as a body will not lose your trust and confidence in me without very good reasons and the evidence for them?

Q. Can I be assured that your need to address any criticism of me/ allegation against me won't mean that you forget my unblemished track-record and everything I have done over the years that has earned your trust and support?

Q. *How will I know that you are still behind me if I am required to be suspended and you are not permitted to talk to me?*

Q. *Will you agree to keep in touch and keep me informed as much as the situation allows?*

Q. *Can I feel assured that you won't allow any knee-jerk reaction by the LA or equivalent authority to jeopardise our relationship, and that you will challenge any action that you consider unjustified?*

Q. *Can I feel assured that you won't allow the LA or Trust to forget my service record or treat me as if I had somehow metamorphosed into a quite different person?*

The latter is a common fear among headteachers suspended or on 'garden leave'. They fear that others will now revise their view of them, usually to their detriment, perhaps thinking that they 'got them wrong', having thought they were really good headteachers and good people, but now see that they weren't.

In summary form, the covenant the headteacher seeks might express the following sentiments, though not necessarily in the same words:

Can I rest assured that if I'm ever embattled, you will keep faith with me until/unless you have compelling reasons not to, continue to fulfil a duty of care and, if you retain confidence in me, stand up for and by me? I'd like to know that you will keep me and my best interests in mind even when I'm not in sight and/or others turn against me.

Covenant framing: the governing body's perspective

Q. *Can we be certain that you will let us know as soon as possible if you do anything that could trigger an allegation or bring the school into disrepute?*

Q. *Can we be assured that you will forewarn us of any potential problems that centre on you or the school and you do not try to cover up anything you shouldn't?*

Q. *Can we be assured that you will never knowingly mislead us or make us think that the blame lies anywhere it doesn't?*

Q. If you should be suspended or similar, can we secure your commitment to continue to act with the same level of integrity and professionalism that you always have, even though we may not be in direct contact with you?

Q. In short, can we be certain that our continuing support of you will be the right thing to do?

If you are a headteacher or governor, then you may choose not to use any of the questions I have formulated here and to reach an understanding in your own way. What's important is to have the intention of coming to an understanding, or formulating a covenant as I have put it. The idea is for the headteacher and governing body to feel that they are operating securely as one with as much mutual trust and as little uncertainty about the relationship as possible.

What is particularly important from the headteacher's point of view is a degree of certainty that s/he won't be ditched without the strongest of reasons. It's a conversation that has to happen before any school-destabilising situation has arisen, so even if it seems awkward and possibly irrelevant to broach the topic when things are going well, that's the time to do it. At or after the event is too late, and may be close to impossible after a suspension has been implemented.

If you need a trigger, then you could allude to the unfortunate experiences of colleague heads and make that the pretext and the context for that conversation.

The covenant might also form part of a broader nurture plan for the headteacher – perhaps for the school leadership team more generally. This is a term I've coined for a plan that seeks to sustain the well-being of the headteacher, initiated by the governing body and bespoke for the specific headteacher. It would clearly need to reflect his/her preferences for support and include any reasonable measures to help the beneficiary to retain energy and commitment. (More details of the Nurture Plan are set out in the Appendix.)

For many headteachers, a key ingredient of the nurture protocol might be a coach or mentor, probably an external and independent consultant in whom the headteacher has confidence and can get the kinds of services s/

he most needs. As someone who has had the privilege of coaching many headteachers, I can attest that those needs vary significantly from head to head. Sometimes it's simply a matter of unburdening. Sometimes it's for what amounts to supervision or the opportunity to talk through ideas and issues. Sometimes it's for something quite different – for a personal development matter (such as improving time or stress management) or for stimulation and fresh thinking.

My strong belief is that every governing body should ask their headteacher:

Would you appreciate the services of a coach that you respect and could turn to for independent support and advice?

In terms of preparing and coping with serious developments, the right coach or mentor can (i) help the headteacher to avoid at least some problem situations, including those that might be occasioned by making poor judgements or failing to take necessary actions, and (ii) be available to support the headteacher though difficult situations that arise.

Sometimes an independent coach (or equivalent) is about the only professionally helpful person a suspended or garden leave school leader can call upon, apart from her/his Union officers.

Step 15: Devise a surge plan

To be a Ready for Anything school, one of the key requirements is a **surge plan**. This is a plan that will enable the school to move from normal operations to the more intense requirements of an exceptional shock event, and to do so as rapidly and smoothly as possible. Unsurprisingly, most schools have measures in place that may contribute to a surge plan (emergency procedures, business continuity plans *etc*) but not necessarily a set of comprehensive arrangements for making a truly significant shift of gear. Trying to make hurried provision for this when something bad happens is not a good idea.

As I've already indicated, schools aren't like hospitals. They don't routinely have to respond to surge events with surge responses. They don't have the same kind of mandate to surge when necessary, except with regard to evacuation requirements. But sometimes they do have to behave like hospitals dealing with a sudden, unexpected influx of say, trauma cases, so it behoves them to figure out the likely arrangements and actions for this before it happens. In the case of schools it won't be the admission of badly injured patients, but it might be the need to deal with a barrage of complaints and enquiries and a media onslaught, or some event that totally shifts the centre of gravity. One option is to self-mandate: commit to having a surge plan and the wherewithal to implement it in response to any event that requires one.

So what does this mean in practice? First and foremost, it requires senior staff and governors to get their heads around the concept of surge capacity. They need to figure out whether the school has sufficient capacity to respond to greater and extraordinary levels of demand and, if not, what needs to happen to create the additional capacity. In a school, that capacity is likely to cover staff, structures, systems and, sometimes, stuff (resources, equipment and rooms and other spaces).

Staff capacity is likely to be the most critical. This depends upon a number of factors, including and ideally having some slack in the system. If in normal modes of operation key staff members are working at full stretch, then there is very little capacity to 'make' extra time to deal with additional demands. Most schools aren't in the happy position of being able to give their staff members lashings of unallocated time to respond to the unexpected, and excessive capacity (more than required even in a crisis) is expensive and wasteful. But it is always important to look at the possibility of building in more contingency time for key players (*eg* the head, maybe the Business Manager, the Media Manager *etc*) which can always be usefully deployed all those times a major response is not required.

The more realistic option is thinking through release time and arrangements, so that those staff members can switch from normal duties to those required for responding to shock events. Role-switching and duty-delegation happen in all schools, but usually temporarily. In major response situations this may need to be a more long-term arrangement, so all concerned may need to be fully up to speed on what will be required of them *in extremis*. Thought should also be given to whether on-going support (and possible remuneration changes) will be needed for staff carrying out unfamiliar roles and for those on the front line of dealing with the extraordinary situation.

Sustainability can also be an issue in a protracted shock-to-the-system situation; a sustained surge can take its toll on those directly involved or implicated, on the school's normal business and on its improvement priorities. The surge plan will need to build in contingency planning – Plan Cs, as it were – including sources of possible reserve capacity, such as additional temporary staff or helpers. It will also include provision for re-prioritising, reviewing what stays live and what has to be suspended or dropped from the school's Major Things To Do List.

Surge capacity issues will also apply to the school's structures and systems. For example, there may need to be: (i) the capacity to accommodate many more meetings of key personnel (perhaps requiring fewer standard meetings); (ii) a special space set aside to house these and the whole response operations; and (iii) additional communication requirements (*eg* regular briefings) as well as possibly new 'rules' about communicating with the 'outside world'.

Given that there will always be unknowns in exceptional events, including the nature of the event itself until it manifests, it is impossible to devise a surge plan that will apply to and cover all eventualities. But talk to those who have been involved in dealing with shock events and they will tell you that things would have gone more smoothly and been less stressful had they been more surge-ready. Having a surge plan will ensure at least a degree of readiness to go up a gear whatever the cause and whenever it's required.

Chapter Four: Response Management Plan

Wise school leaders know that there's a limit to the things they can control; the world is too complex and there are too many unknowns to anticipate and neutralise every possible threat. All the preventative and planning measures in the world might not be enough to stop a really nasty development occurring. So now we turn attention to what action might be appropriate if it should.

What might be the catalyst or early indication of something that turns out to be school-destabilising?

These are some that I have encountered:

- A phone call from a panicking teacher on a school trip
- A Twitter storm about something school-related
- The sudden, unexpected arrival of figures with the authority to suspend the headteacher
- An out-of-the-blue phone call from a local or national newspaper
- An email or letter that turns out to be a letter 'bomb'

As I indicated early on, it could be a seemingly minor matter – a routine parental complaint, for example – that for various reasons escalates into something altogether more serious. The truth is, not all crises start off as obvious crises. This does not mean that you need to be on hyper-alert mode or perpetually paranoid, just that you should act with awareness, as much wisdom as you can and probably err on the side of more rather than less caution.

Needless to say, every situation is different. No two developments are identical, have the same profile or take precisely the same trajectory, so it's not possible to list a set of prescriptions that apply to all situations. The suggestions that follow reflect what I hope has proved good practice (I won't claim best practice) in the situations I have been involved in, and I hope that many will be relevant to those in which many school leaders find themselves, but they don't purport to cover everything or be relevant to all situations. That's just not possible.

With these caveats in mind, let's begin the response management process.

So: You've received some information. You know or suspect that it might be significant.

A first step is to determine whether you are the first and only person to have received it.

Lots of problems occur nowadays because the critical information is already 'out there'. If you have a Tell Us First policy, and it has been kept, then (depending on the precipitating incident) you should be at least one of the first to know about it and you will know who else might know. If it has not been kept, then find out who else does know; this will affect your future actions.

If you sense that it has the potential to explode or spread, then secure a promise to let you investigate or take other necessary action before any further action is taken by the source.

BE CAUTIOUS in making your initial response:

- Showing the need for caution and understanding priority are usually strong indicators of good judgement – which is what you need buckets of in response management
- Say nothing that could be precipitant, incriminating or that you might later come to regret
- SAY LESS RATHER THAN MORE

Of course, shock-to-the-system events can kick off in a variety of ways, and not necessarily with the head/school hearing about something. On occasions, it can even start with authority figures turning up at the school and insisting that the headteacher leaves the premises immediately – a truly shocking development, especially if this is the first time the head has any idea that s/he is the subject of an allegation or similar.

When this happens, one very important self-protective action the school leader needs to take is to ensure that anything s/he leaves the school with is logged and validated by the authority figures and/or senior staff members (such as the school's business manager). This will include documentation and hardware, such as school laptops, and also keys and other security information. This action will ensure that s/he cannot be accused subsequently of removing evidence or any other materials that could count against him/her or form part of any investigation.

It will also ensure that the school is not massively inconvenienced by the lack of access to key kinds of data or to security systems. Apart from the problems that this can cause to the smooth running of the school in the school leader's absence, it does little to dispose staff and governors kindly to him or her. And the last thing the school leader wants at this time is his/her staff huffing and puffing, particularly if they are going to be contributing to an investigation. It's just not the ideal state for them to be in, even if it doesn't materially affect the substance of those contributions.

As for school leaders, they need to think carefully about what school-related information they have at home and whether it could put them in any compromising or vulnerable positions if anything 'goes wrong'. Having clear guidelines on this for the staff in general is also important. Ensuring the accessibility of key school data and documents to those who may need them in unforeseen circumstances is something that all school leaders need to prepare for. Just how crucial this can be is attested in **The Third Headteacher's Tale** in the final section of this book).

Acknowledge, but probably don't admit

If the situation involves someone presenting in a seemingly distressed, agitated or angry state, then acknowledge the other's state or concern

(*'This is obviously of real concern for you'*) or the seeming seriousness of an event (*'This looks as if it could be a serious matter'*), but don't admit or attribute culpability at this stage. This is usually the best early-stage response principle. Admissions can come later if necessary.

Be very careful about using the word 'sorry' in case it is taken as an admission of guilt and/or an apology when you are not meaning it to be. Even something as seemingly benign as *'I'm sorry that this has happened'* can be heard or intentionally misconstrued as an admission that the school is at fault.

Minimal Necessary Response: consider making this your default response principle

I've found that this is often proves an excellent guiding principle: saying no more than you really need to, and saying less rather than more. In an anxious or worked-up emotional state, it is very easy to talk loosely and freely. And it can be tempting to emote expressively and immoderately, jump to conclusions about who is to blame and say things that too quickly lock onto a particular definition of the situation – what psychologists call a premature cognitive commitment. Before you really understand the situation with which you are faced, even being too fulsomely empathic can create problems down the line. As indicated above, even a well-intentioned statement such *'I'm so sorry that this has happened to your son'* can all-too-easily be construed – wilfully or otherwise – as an admission of culpability. As a rule, keep verbal responses low-key and deflationary and as brief as necessary.

How you present, as well as what you say, is also important. A minimal emotional response is also usually the safest one. That is, come across as emotionally neutral but concerned, though calibrate according to your reading of the situation. If, say, children have been injured, then emotional neutrality will sound too much like heartless indifference. You'll need to tweak the emotional dial up or down according to your judgement of the sensitivities of the situation, but adjust it upwards no more than you have to. See Panel 10 for some examples of minimal necessary responses (MNRs).

Use holding responses

If you've only just heard about a potentially critical incident, then it's best to use a holding response until you are sufficiently informed and certain of the facts to say anything more specific. For example:

'I've only just heard about this myself. I'll respond when I know more details.'

'I'm sure you'll hear just as soon as possible.'

It makes sense to advise all staff members to refer enquiries to you (the headteacher) or the Media Manager. They should be told to do this in relation to any incident that could prove sensitive or potentially damaging and about which they do not have the authority to speak on behalf of the school. So:

'You'll have to ask the head.'

Advise them **not** to respond with something such as:

'I'm sorry, I wish I could tell you more, but I can't. You'll have to ask the head'

This formulation implies that the staff member knows more than s/he is willing to give away or that s/he is being silenced. It won't endear him/her to the enquiring party and s/he may come under pressure to reveal more than she should.

The challenge is to keep the response concise and non-committal (until a full statement can be given with confidence) and yet not appear uncaring, indifferent or defensive. But in the bigger scheme of things, better to come across unfavourably at that moment than to say something that does more harm than good and can never be retracted. A well-intentioned but unauthorised spokesperson can do just this – more harm than good.

A level of self-awareness is very useful in situations of uncertainty as it is in so many others. If you know you tend to 'talk too much', and especially if you are aware of having a strong approval driver, then you might need to make a very conscious effort not to say more than you absolutely have to and in a form you might not naturally use. Remind yourself that being liked at this moment is not the priority. It's a reminder you might have to give yourself frequently on the challenging journey ahead.

Panel 10

Minimal Necessary Responses

- *'OK. We'll look into it.'*
- *'This sounds as if it could be too important to respond to hastily or off the cuff. We'll investigate and get back to you within 48 hours.'*
- *'Thank you for bringing this to my attention. It sounds concerning. We'll handle it immediately.'*
- *'Can we keep this between ourselves until I can gather together the other senior leaders and trustees and we can decide how best to respond?'*
- *'I'd like to know the precise reason I am being suspended.'*

Do whatever you say you are going to do

If you want to retain the trust, cooperation and good-will (assuming you have them) of whomever you are dealing with, then keep your promises. Completing circuits of communication is an obvious case in point. If you say, *'We will get back to you'*, then get back to them as and when promised. A response window of 48 hours might be your default.

Forty eight hours usually allows enough time for at least a preliminary investigation without being unduly rushed, and you can provide an update even if you cannot say anything definite or conclusive at the end of the 48 hours.

So many organisations do not do what they say they are going to do. They say, for example, that they will return a phone call but don't. Many of the parents and other people schools deal with will have had countless experiences of broken promises from those in authority or some organisation or another and may be predisposed to expect the same infuriating and frustrating treatment from a school (especially if their contact with it is normally minimal).

It's amazing how many 'brownie points' a school can garner if it bucks the trend and actually does what it says it will do. So, make sure that all staff abide by the keeping promises policy you should have in place.

If you are personally on the other end of the communication line – the subject of the crisis situation rather than the one dealing with it – then it's up to you to ask: *'When exactly can I expect a response or decision?'*. Or, if you won't be getting a definitive decision any time soon, to ask when, how often and from whom will you be getting updates of the situation and how things are progressing.

Anyone suspended or on 'garden leave' should be told these things, but often they are not, so asking will serve to prime those responsible.

Determine any policy violation and investigate effectively, efficiently and ethically

This will not always be a relevant step, of course, but very often a situation blows up because a policy has not been adhered to. You will need to investigate to determine any violation to or departure from official school policy – the level, the nature and the culpable party. As some of the MNR examples above indicate, say nothing before the investigation that could pre-empt its findings.

If you sanction an investigation, then make sure that it is conducted by an appropriately qualified and independent person, that it is as rigorous as it needs to be, that the investigator documents contributions and evidence and that nothing contaminates it or adversely affects the integrity with which it is carried out. Also, try to ensure that it takes no longer than necessary. Investigations perceived as unnecessarily or even deliberately protracted are sources of great frustration and often of anger and suspicion. They almost always aggravate the situation.

All this sounds so very obvious, and yet I have encountered investigations that have fallen short on all the above criteria. Sloppy or even rigged investigations do more harm than good. So do those carried out by people with their own vested interests in skewing them or protracting them.

One investigation into a suspended headteacher took such an outrageously long time that it was impossible not to suspect that the independent HR consultant who carried it out was either on the make (*ie* spinning it out to earn more money) or in the palm of those who commissioned him. Another suspicion of the same consultant was that he protracted the investigation largely through fishing in areas where he shouldn't have been fishing at all. It's important that every investigation keeps focused, doesn't stray from its brief and that if 'other things' come to light, then these are the inevitable result of scrutiny in legitimate areas not speculative sorties or ill-intended mission creep.

One of the other fairly common but unforgiveable traps that inexperienced investigators can fall into is giving too much information to the person under investigation. Here is an extract from an email by a school leader under investigation at the time of writing. This headteacher knows that she is both completely innocent of the matter for which she is being charged and that the whole process is being mishandled:

'The mishandling part is the fact I've been told all the details (or most) despite it being an investigation into my conduct. Madness! But to my favour it helps me that I know what I'm dealing with and there are no uncertainties.'

This school leader is aware that an investigation handled in a ham-fisted manner will not stand up to scrutiny. If it ever reaches the stage of a hearing/tribunal, then the incompetent way in which the investigation was conducted will play in her favour.

My experience is that, for an innocent school leader at the centre of an investigation, an investigation that is badly handled is deeply frustrating and infuriating at the time, but can be a blessing when the investigation process itself comes under the spotlight.

Assess priority

This is a concurrent rather than consecutive step. Make a provisional judgement of the importance and seriousness of the issue. This will help you work out what level of resources to allocate to the matter and how to present the matter and your response to the world.

Better usually to err on the side of over-estimating rather than under-estimating its priority. One of the benefits of this is showing that the matter is being taken seriously. Also, if it does escalate, then you are already geared up to match the resources required.

If you want to approach priority assessment in a very systematic way, then consider having a 1-10 scale, possibly one in line with, say, the Risk Matrix (if you have one, and schools often do) in the Business Continuity Plan.

By the way, the more you can do things systematically and methodically, the better. In a tumultuous situation, whatever you can turn into a calm routine, do so. It reduces anxiety, helps with mood management and helps you to feel that you can regulate and control things – at least to some degree.

Assessing priority and seriousness is obviously not a one-off action. It will need to be done frequently. Some issues escalate suddenly or exponentially and the resource allocation will need to match it.

Bring together the 'Critical Few'

In readiness for dealing with the kind of shock-to-the-system development we're concerned with in this book, it makes sense for each school to decide the composition of the body that is likely to be responsible for making the key decisions and for the strategic planning of the school's response – if that is not too grand a term. It's the school's equivalent of the UK government's emergency planning committee (the Cobra Committee).

Ideally, this should be agreed before the school is hit with something serious. It will almost certainly include senior leaders and governors and/or trustee representatives, probably those with particular areas of expertise (*eg* in HR). The Media Manager will almost certainly be a member, as will the headteacher and Chair of Governors and CEO (if it's part of a Multi-Academy Trust) unless any of these individuals is the focus of the issue concerned.

One possible name for this steering and decision-making group is the Response Management Leadership Team (RMLT). I shall use the term from now on.

Leading the RMLT

In my experience, whoever leads the RMLT has two critical jobs to do with the team other than agreeing decisions and actions. The first is ensuring that meetings are conducted in a state of moderate vigour. That is, they are conducted with enough mental and emotional energy to facilitate quality thinking and get things sorted, but insufficient to create high levels of anxiety or other unhelpful emotions – fury, exasperation, indignation *etc.* The second is to ensure that the team doesn't turn meetings into dramas to feed their ego hungers – especially for recognition and stimulation. In fact, the leader should insist that the team has the mantra, We don't turn crises into dramas, so that it operates as professionally and effectively as it can do, and is about the school, not them.

It's also crucial that the leader insists on confidentiality and/or the importance of keeping to script, *ie* what the team has agreed about what can and can't be said.

As for the business of the RMLT, the two critical questions to confront and agree are almost certainly going to be:

- What exactly has gone wrong?
- What should our response be?

Respond in line with your corporate response style

In an earlier section, we focused upon the importance of having a corporate or house response style. This comes into play here, because whatever the substance of the response, the style should be consistent with the organisational self-image – your preferred and default way of coming across. Ideally, for parents and others this will be recognisably the school as it normally is, just with tonal adjustments to reflect the level of seriousness. So if the school normally presents as a friendly place, then the language and manner of anything you present shouldn't suddenly seem very formal and bureaucratic. If it does, then it will make the school seem strange and risk estranging those who usually feel comfortable with it. Psychologists would recognise this as preserving constancy.

Match the response strategy to the nature of the precipitating event and level of culpability

Deciding the response strategy will be a critical and probably a defining and determining moment in the development of the whole situation.

Although there is a spectrum of possible responses, they usually reflect one of two broad directions. Which is taken depends mainly upon your answer to the following crucial question:

How culpable are you/we/the school?

If the answer is 'wholly' or 'very', then the broad response strategy is likely to be: 'We need to come clean'.

This is the **It's Down To Us Big Time Strategy.**

If the answer is: 'very little' or 'not at all', then the response strategy is likely to be: 'Initially, say the minimum necessary'.

This is the **Minimal Culpability Strategy.**

It's Down To Us Big Time

This is likely to be used for a self-inflicted injury, a scandal or a crisis that could have been avoided. Examples include:

- An inappropriate relationship
- Financial irregularities
- The headteacher's poor 'provision of services' for the governing body
- Cheating and fabricating (data, exams *etc*)
- Staff actions that seriously violate school policy
- Negligence on a school trip (that does go or could have gone badly wrong)
- Staff members playing truant!
- A cover-up
- Failure to tackle school-based problems in a timely and effective way

The 'It's down to us' direction is a *mea culpa* acceptance of responsibility strategy. It's coming clean and promising to clean up. It means not seeking to deny wrongdoing or ineptitude, not covering up or minimising the significance of what's happened. It's committing to get to the bottom of the situation and ensuring that it never happens again. In time, it is coming up with a convincing plan to make this happen.

Nowadays this is generally accepted as the most successful as well as the most ethical response strategy. It certainly wasn't at one time. Until fairly recently, legal and other advisers would often advise their culpable clients to keep schtum, own up to nothing, play down the significance of the matter and conceal and dissemble for as long as possible until they have worked out how best to spin it. Shock-to-the-system developments in some of the world's biggest or best known companies (VW, BP, United Airlines *etc*) have shown that not coming out and coming clean when something has gone badly wrong is not a response that can work nowadays, especially given social media and accessibility to information. Besides, it is clearly a morally compromised response.

It's also a response that comes from spin, and generally people nowadays react badly to it.

If you and your school have done everything possible to prevent school-harming events occurring, then you should hope never to be in the situation of accepting full responsibility for a major wrongdoing. There are situations, however, in which you may be: situations in which you have to apologise and accept responsibility for something you caused but unavoidably or unwittingly so. That is, you've just been very unlucky. The equivalent in the corporate world is a food manufacturer who unknowingly puts out contaminated food products despite complying with all legal, H&S and environmental health procedures.

Minimal culpability

This is the appropriate response strategy when you or your school bear little or no responsibility for anything that has happened. Examples include:

- False or vexatious allegations
- Truth distortions and misrepresentations
- Mountains being made out of molehills
- You as a scape-goat or fall guy
- Events with serious consequences over which you had no control

The approach here is to respond in a restrained, cautious but appropriately robust way, and to take the situation as seriously as you judge it to deserve.

As a rule of thumb, then:

If you have screwed up, then err on the side of effusiveness.

If you haven't, then err on the side of robust restraint.

If you are at most only minimally culpable for anything that has occurred, then keep any statements you make crisp and concise, in line with the minimal necessary response principle. Why? Because the more detail you go into, the greater the potential risks, especially at an early stage of a developing situation.

As an example, consider the problems a school can get from the way it handles an incident of poor pupil behaviour. The school may have acted reasonably or even impeccably, but in a face-to-face exchange with outraged parents bent on making unacceptable demands or intent on escalating the situation, it can be easy to 'say too much' that only inflames the situation.

In reality, many behaviour issues can be handled by the 'disruption to learning' bit of the policy, and be left at that. For example, if parents are seriously riled by the sanctions the school imposed on a pupil for an in-class act of misbehaviour, then instead of getting bogged down in arguments over the precise details of the incident, the response might be:

'The truth is that Jamie's behaviour disrupted his own learning and that of others in the class. As our behaviour policy makes clear, no behaviour is acceptable if it disrupts learning for the child concerned or the children affected.'

If something like this is said, and repeated if necessary – the 'broken record' assertiveness strategy – then it will prevent the exploration of further areas of contention. Getting into detailed explanations and defences can be a rocky path to go down. This approach could be construed as being economical with the truth; I think it's just sensibly focusing on what is key – and unarguable.

There's another powerful reason for keeping responses concise:

You rarely need many words to tell the truth.

Agree a communications strategy

The content part of the communications strategy is the answer to two questions:

What exactly are we going to be saying when we respond?

Are we going to have the same response for all recipients?

In other words, are we going to say exactly the same thing using the same words to all our audiences – staff, parents, governors, the local authority, the press *etc*?

While it might seem sensible to make adjustments to the message in line with each particular audience and our relationship with it, there are dangers in this. Hearing or seeing different versions can be misconstrued and create suspicions, so one principle to consider is **minimal message deformation**, *ie* make no more adjustments than you feel you really have to.

The other part of the communications strategy concerns the form(s) in which you are going to present formal responses. Is it going to be a written statement, a written statement read out loud, an interview, an email, a message on social media, a combination of these or something else?

Each form has its pros and cons.

It is often best to avoid an interview or question/answer situation unless the Media Manager/spokesperson is trained and confident. If providing a written statement, decide beforehand whether questions are to be taken and then stick to it. Not taking questions can appear cold, detached or even evasive, but it can prevent unfortunate elaboration and comments that unwittingly aggravate the situation.

Agreeing action

The RMLT will need to consider how to respond to the situation it is confronted with. One legitimate option is **Take No Action** (at present).

This is the most minimal of all minimal necessary responses, but it can be the right one, especially when there is a good chance of dissolution before the need for resolution. Wise school leaders know that a 'wait and see' approach often makes more sense than rushing in with all guns blazing. For example, a wise head may sense that a very angry email from an irate parent may amount to nothing if it was simply someone getting something off their chest, sent late in the evening and possibly fuelled by a glass or two.

Non-action (which deciding not to act is) is very different from inaction. Inaction is not taking action when it may need to be taken. It is usually passivity, procrastination, diffidence or denial. It's never the right response because it's a failure to make a decision.

Non-action is also a legitimate response at a much later stage in the response process: after an investigation when you are confident of where you stand and all required response statements have been made. For example, if a serious complaint has been fully investigated and the result and conclusion made clear, then there is no requirement to acknowledge let alone respond to anyone who persists in complaining.

The alternative to the legitimate response of Non-action is, of course, the legitimate response of Action.

Version two, as it were, of the minimal necessary response course of action might be described as the **Short Shrift response** – an assertive, robust rejoinder. It can sound curt and cold, but it also implies: this is the plain and simple truth. For example:

The Trustees and leadership want to make it quite clear that no policy has been broken.

Our data are presented in line with legal/Ofsted requirements, and the advice from the local authority about putting 'our best foot forward'. There has absolutely been no falsification of data.

The alternative, version three of the minimal necessary response, is an **Expansively Minimal Response.** You might choose this option if you really do have a lot that needs to be said. This is a more substantial, and probably highly careful, cautious and nuanced response. It may also be a more provisional and tentative one. If that's the case, then it should be made clear so as to obviate the need for any retraction later on.

Retractions are almost always bad news. Avoid them whenever possible.

Here's an example of an expansive minimal response

'We want to update you on the investigation into the playground incident involving two Y6 pupils. First an update on the girls themselves. Aisha Wallace has made an excellent recovery and we expect her to be fit enough to return to school by the end of this week. Stacie Gordon is still poorly and we wish her a speedy recovery. We have placed the technical part of the investigation into the hands of an independent buildings surveyor. He has our school records which show that the wall has been subject to the proper health and safety checks. Contrary to stories now circulating, there are no records of anyone having raised any concerns about the soundness of the wall. An investigation has been launched into the school's handling of the incident. This is also being undertaken by an independent consultant. Until both investigations have been completed there is nothing more we can say with any confidence. We will do so as soon as we can. Thank you.'

However substantial the response, it should again be no more substantial than it needs be. As a rule, the lengthier the verbal response, the greater the possibility of saying something that you come to regret. Saying more than you really need to is a temptation to be avoided at an early stage of a developing situation. The exception is likely to be when basic facts (*eg* about casualty numbers) account for the length of the statement.

So, to sum up, there are three legitimate versions of a minimal necessary response reflecting different judgements about the situation and what is required:

Version one: No Response (at least at 'this' time)

Version two: Short Shrift (brief and emphatic)

Version three: Expansively minimal (more detailed, more nuanced but still cautious and as minimal as possible)

Other action

I've focused on verbal action, but of course there may be physical actions to take as well. Investigations will often be one of them. I've said already how important it is to ensure these are conducted competently, and that those that don't secure the confidence of those concerned can (to repeat a phrase I've used often) do more harm than good.

It's hard to say much about other actions because these are necessarily situation-specific. But recall a point made in the section on prevention: the more that actions are in line with the normal culture and systems of the school, the more successful they are likely to prove. You still want to appear to be the same school or the same person as you always have been, just adjusting action to a new and unusual set of circumstances. Start to act in ways which seem totally out of character, and you risk losing the support and trust of those you most need it from.

For example, if your school is normally open and welcoming, don't suddenly start to be secretive and unwelcoming just because of one bad experience. If you care for your pupils every day, then be the primary care-givers if something traumatic happens; don't automatically sub-contract the main caring function to outside counsellors and psychologists. The principle to guide action here is:

Stay familiar even in unfamiliar circumstances.

The other obvious principle for determining appropriate action is to follow the procedures that you already have in place for extraordinary developments: crisis management and business continuity plans, for example. In the heat and turmoil of a shock-to-the-system event, it can be easy to get disorientated and 'forget' what you have already planned for.

Linked to this is the encouragement that can be derived from bringing to mind reference experiences. That is, recall times when you have successfully dealt with difficult incidents and take encouragement from them. So when you appear to be entering new worlds of experience, remind yourself of the second guiding principle: **We know more than we don't know.** You'll know, for example, about relationships between staff, about who is good at doing what, and about typical patterns of behaviour. This knowledge will help you decide the right actions to take.

Will this be the end of the matter?

A swift, clear, assertive response may result in a swift and satisfactory end to the matter. A confident statement following a brief investigation that has, say, not upheld an allegation, might also be enough to draw a line under things. But often this will not be the case, which is why more and more incidents or developments are having disproportionate effects. Your first response may have to be one of many. This is likely to be the case if:

i.   The issue is complex, needs a lengthy investigation, including by external authorities, or has its own life-cycle (as, for example, traumatic bereavement situations tend to: ending them quickly can seem callous and provoke a backlash).

ii. You are subject to an ineptly managed investigation. (Many of the school leaders I have worked with have found themselves caught up in a process that seems to drift or drag on inexplicably. Their reasonable assumptions are that those behind it are floundering, 'making it up as they go along', 'digging themselves into a hole' or 'clueless' about how to bring it to a close. Given their mix of emotions – frustration, bewilderment, uncertainty – and, above all, their lack of confidence in the perpetrators, the school leaders concerned often contribute to the protraction because they are determined not to allow the process to end unsatisfactorily or because they quite rightly want to intervene to influence the progress of the investigation.)

iii. Your initial responses as the person or team in charge were misjudged or aggravating.

iv. The situation is a developing one.

v.   Others are seeking to benefit from and so intent on keeping the process alive, even more so if they have no genuine interest in resolution or closure.

With regard to the last point, understand this:

If one avenue is closed to them, then the determined agitator will always seek another and, if necessary, another and another.

That is, those bent on pursuing their project will not rest until they have tried everything possible, and perhaps not even then. That has certainly been the experience of many schools. All kinds of strategies can be deployed to this end, including relentless freedom of information requests and attempts to garner support from any remotely interested party or organisation. Local Authority not interested? Try Ofsted. Little joy from Ofsted? Try the Department for Education. Little interest there? Try the Information Commissioners Office…and so on.

Subsequent responses

For each new development, the question to address is:

What should our/my response be now?

In coming to a judgement, the key determinant is how much change there is to the situation.

Is the situation largely a static one, perhaps resulting from a one-off event that is now over and in the past, and with no new developments or information coming to light?

If so, the subsequent responses may well be the same responses you have already made.

Why? For the simple but powerful reason that it implies the truth is already out there. Also, because consistency of message is usually perceived favourably, even if the message itself is not very palatable.

Is the situation an evolving one?

If this is the case, if the situation is developing and dynamic, then often the best response is:

Provide updates, but the minimum required and with the least possible modification to the initial response.

Why? Because while updates show that you are 'on the case' and intent on putting the truth out there, both departures and elaborations from the initial message can raise suspicions. Some respondents might think that you are changing your story rather than providing updated and increasingly more accurate versions of the same story. It's a response consistent with the minimal message deformation principle.

So the school leader or the RMLT should keep asking: *What response now?*

And, more specifically: *Does it really need to be a different one?*

Response management competences

In practical terms, the chief organisational competences are probably prioritising and scheduling. The first one is a judgement about what should come first and about sequencing according to importance and urgency. The second is about ensuring that priorities are translated into action. The tools here are a prioritised 'things to do' list converted into an action plan. (See Panel 11 for an example of this.)

There are also **psycho-emotional competences** and, in some circumstances, they can be absolutely critical. This certainly applies to crises directly involving or affecting pupils and/or their families or staff members. I've very deliberately not over-concentrated on these kinds of incidents because they tend to be ones that schools have always known they might have to deal with and should have prepared for in their crisis planning arrangements. I'm thinking of such awful incidents as road traffic accidents, deaths on school journeys, floods and other natural disasters and high-profile disasters such as the Grenfell Tower fire.

Nonetheless, it would be appropriate to highlight some of the problems schools can create for themselves if their responses are psycho-emotionally inept, insensitive or plain non-existent. I'm going to re-frame most of these failures as the actions schools should take to be psycho-emotionally competent responders.

- Prime staff to identify and properly interpret unusual patterns of pupil behaviour as troubled rather than simply troublesome. If pupils have been traumatised then their behaviour will reflect this. Different pupils behave differently, but typical symptoms of distress and disturbance include sleep deprivation, a loss of concentration, hyperactivity, making strange noises, snatching and stealing objects and obsessing about things, as well as acts of what might seem like wilful misbehaviour. Understanding and responding to these as presenting behaviours of troubled states will avoid inviting (justified) complaints from parents as well as being the right thing to do for the pupils concerned.
- Prime staff to be vigilant for the potentially vulnerable, and to avoid narrowly defining vulnerability. That means priming staff

not to interpret the seemingly normal behaviour of some pupils following a traumatic incident as indifference or immunity. They may well be affected but in a state of (probably temporary) numbness. Prime staff also not to be surprised if numbness modulates into something harder to deal with – anger, for example. What applies to pupils applies equally to staff members if the situation relates to them.

- Prime staff not to force children to talk about their troubling or traumatising experiences. Some may want to, some may not or not at any particular time. Ensure staff members don't seek to meet their own needs by requiring children to talk if that's not what they want to do. Again, for 'pupils' read 'staff' if they are at the centre of things.

- If possible, provide staff with any additional training they may need for responding to difficult issues and being strong and caring 'containers' for their pupils. These competences ought to have been part of the schools resilience-building programme for staff undertaken as part of the Preparation Management Plan.

- If possible, provide as an option specialist help for those who need and want it. However, if staff members normally have excellent competent carer-type relationships with pupils, then bringing in professional strangers may not always be necessary or the best thing to do. Occasionally, well-intentioned outsiders may do harm as well as good, especially if insufficiently briefed, so that they may present additional problems for the school at a time when it is already fully stretched on the emotional labour front.

- Ensure that no pupil, family or teacher gets the message that 'out of sight is out of mind'. For example, if a pupil is at home or in hospital following a nasty accident, then make sure that the school stays in contact with the child and the family as much as they require or would value. This might include visits to explore any concerns – for example, about work that is being missed, examinations that might be affected or how the child will manage and be perceived (if injured, for instance) when s/he returns to school. Plan for and talk about re-entry and ensure arrangements are as sensitively conceived as possible.

- Prime staff about re-entry arrangements. For example, ensure that staff seek a bespoke approach to catching up or varying demands for pupils. Some pupils may not be able to cope with the pressures of 'normal' work for some time. Others may want to immerse themselves in the safety and normality of school work, so might not appreciate a 'go easy' approach.

- Ensure that there are opportunities for pupils who are traumatised or who have suffered in some way to have time out, time alone or some other sanctuary arrangement. The same may apply to staff members.

- Prime staff to take account of the curricular sensitivities of troubled pupils. If a traumatising incident has involved the death or serious injury of pupils, then it may be obvious that curriculum content focusing on death may be troubling. But curriculum sensitivities may be more oblique and subtle. Children may find work on addition and subtraction difficult, even if the resonance is sub-conscious, though some may gain comfort in the apparent closed-world certainties of mathematics. Asking children to write about their experiences might be a problem for some. Work on time-lines or particular places with painful reminders can also prove problematic. Not forcing pupils to engage with content that is obviously and seriously distressing for them may be emotionally intelligent and will also obviate the need to deal with the understandable wrath of protective parents/carers.

- Be wary about what information you share and who it is shared with. Inappropriate disclosures or disclosures to those who may not use the information wisely may lead to a loss of trust on the part of those it concerns (*eg* parents) and a lot worse than this. On the other hand, there may be serious repercussions if sensitive information is not shared with those with a need to know – with relevant teachers, for instance.

- Finally, be alert to significant anniversaries. Parents may expect the school to remember and mark the anniversary of an incident that was meaningful for them. Not doing so can provoke the kind of outrage that can nowadays spread quickly and widely on social media. But marking an anniversary in an acceptable way is also important, so checking with those most directly concerned about what they would regard as appropriate is equally necessary.

Panel 11

On 23rd May 2016, a number of schools in England received anonymous phone calls to say that bombs had been planted on school premises. Most received three such calls. The headteacher of one secondary school at which students in Years 11, 12 and 13 were sitting examinations took the following actions:

1. Staff were told about the call.
2. All students (including those sitting exams) were evacuated to a school field. All but the exam students were sent home when it began to rain heavily.
3. Checks were made to account for all pupils.
4. The police were alerted.
5. The exam boards were notified and guidance sought.
6. Pupils involved in exams were placed in an area (the tennis hall) where there was least noise and disturbance (presumably after a search of the premises).
7. Parents were sent a text message: '*We have evacuated the school with police agreement following three phone calls regarding an explosive device. Lessons will resume tomorrow.*'

Keep staff informed but not overwhelmed

Generally speaking, it's good to provide staff with updates but this has to be done without adversely affecting their psycho-emotional states. The school is not well served by staff who are anxious but powerless. Updates and briefings will also help them to continue playing any useful parts they can and to be sensitive to the demands being made on senior staff.

Proactive Anticipation: Preparing for what might lie ahead

The RMLT will need to use whatever information it has to consider the likely trajectory of the mature-stage situation. There are three main possibilities:

i. A satisfactory closure

ii. A false peace or lull before the storm

iii. A protracted rollercoaster

My experience is that for a shock-to-the-system development, a reasonably quick and satisfactory closure with no more fall-out is possible but less likely than a false peace or another 'attack' stage. This is certainly the case if the catalyst for the situation is someone intent on escalation or a determined trouble-maker or individual/group with an axe to grind and intent on wielding it again. If you are centre-stage/the focus of the situation, then you can expect a personal rollercoaster.

As regards the impact of a career-derailing event on a school leader, the trajectory that I have observed several times is broadly a three-phase one:

Shock – Slump – Mobilising Outrage

If you are a school leader who has suddenly been falsely accused of something serious or frog-marched from your premises by authority figures who have suspended you, then shock is an understandable initial reaction. If you are then forced into a kind of solitary isolation with very little contact with anyone from your school, then it is likely that you will experience a slump of energy and feel very low. This will be especially acute if you also feel deserted by colleagues within your network who you thought would at least have you in mind.

But later, if and when you begin to sense the perceived injustice of what has happened to you – assuming that you are largely innocent of any charges *etc* – then you may be mobilised by that outrage to take action that will move you forward. That action is likely to include securing the support of your professional association and perhaps securing the services of a solicitor. Being angry is fine, but it needs to be channelled towards appropriate action, not allowed to eat away at you.

There are, of course, other possible emotional sequences, some of them complex and even ambivalent. If you are being investigated but remain in post and in school, then you may be trying to manage a mix of anger, fear, humiliation and, if you sense that the whole thing is being mismanaged, bitter-sweet detachment.

One of the keys to surviving in this situation is to let the process take its course and just get on with the day job. If you feel outraged by the situation you are in or the way things are being handled, then it isn't easy to resist the temptation to intervene, protest or display emotions you may later come to regret. The school leaders who have most impressed me are those who have remained dignified and kept their emotions in check, so much so that sometimes most others in the school didn't know that anything was amiss.

Encountering the strategically unpleasable

Some shock-to-the-system developments can persist for a year or more. Worse still, it can seem like the postponement of any final or satisfactory outcome. Not knowing for certain whether or not a horrible experience is finally over is a stressful, unfinished business type of experience. I've witnessed it up-close, and it takes its toll.

The endless dragging-on situation can happen for several reasons. One is that the conduct of the investigation is inept. Those who initiate it may know that it is drifting or veering off-course, but they allow that to happen because they are floundering (*ie* they don't know how to close it) or, even worse, are seeking to secure a preferred outcome. But the most common reason for the non-termination of a situation is that those provoking it don't want to bring it to a close, or want something more than they want a reasonable and mutually acceptable outcome. I call these the **strategically unpleasable**.

There's almost nothing you can do to satisfy the strategically unpleasable. Their motives are sometimes easy to surmise (*eg* financial gain) but often they are not obvious or straightforward. It sometimes seems that they are seeking to meet personal needs – for recognition, stimulation and power, for example – and that they will go on doing so as long as they can. Sometimes the action they are taking looks like their latest project. Look into their past, and you are likely to find that they have prosecuted other similar projects. They have form.

One familiar strategy is attrition: they will persist and persist – with, for example, relentless FOI (freedom of information) requests or intermittent campaigns to try to procure the firepower of major institutions – until they wear down whoever they have their teeth into. It is or it verges on harassment; or it's stalking by another name.

Sometimes, of course, the strategically unpleasable are seriously disturbed or substance-addicted or have other serious issues. Engaging them is hard and usually bruising, and the challenge can be compounded by the very organisations to which schools may turn to for advice and support if those organisations take the line that if you are reasonable with the other party, then they will be reasonable with the school. Assumptions of rationality and reasonableness can be frustrating and infuriating with staff at the sharp end of things. There are people 'out there' who are not at all like this.

What all this can mean in reality is a rollercoaster of highs and lows: of quiet-ish periods and fresh eruptions. This pattern is in my experience more likely than unremittingly high levels of intense activity, but it can be all the more stressful for it. Expecting and waiting for the next development can be even more stressful than dealing with an on-going but known situation.

The RMLT leader has the job of preparing the team – logistically, mentally and emotionally – for the long haul, often a year or more. This is probably a task that also requires and benefits from governing body involvement. Indeed, the key question the governing body will probably need to ask is:

Would you (the headteacher) and/or any other staff directly involved benefit from additional support or adjustments to your duties while this situation is on-going?

Support network contraction

For several of the headteachers that I have worked with, one of the hardest things that they have had to deal with has been a drop off in support from colleague heads. This has usually been gradual, with some initial rallying around and expressions of sympathy, but not always. Depending on their reading of the situation, disassociation by former colleagues can be sudden. It can be experienced by the affected/suspended head as desertion, though they might also understand why this has occurred: self-preservation, fear of contamination by association, just being too consumed with their own school business or a necessary proscription from direct contact. If the latter, then the drawbridge going up is not what the withdrawing heads might have wanted. Nonetheless, it is distressing for those concerned to go from being an esteemed colleague to what seems like a bad smell in a very short period of time. What nearly all the heads in this position have said to me is: '*You soon learn who your true friends are*'.

I have sometimes shared with the heads I have supported the opening lines of a poem, *I Am*, by the 19th-Century poet John Clare. Although Clare's poem alludes to his latter part of life in a mental asylum, the heads' experiences have all resonated with the sentiments:

> *I am! Yet what I am who cares, or knows?*
>
> *My friends forsake me like a memory lost.*
>
> *I am the self-consumer of my woes.*

Of course, not all school leaders trying to manage very challenging situations experience a contraction of their support networks. Some are delighted and buoyed-up by expressions of support from school leader colleagues and others within their network. Some are even surprised by the particular individuals who offer support – especially those who were not regarded as close colleagues. It is a circumstantial variable. But when contraction does happen it can leave those concerned feeling intensely isolated and professionally lonely. They can usually access support from their professional association, but often not as much as they would like or at the times they most need it because of the limited resources of the unions concerned.

I've already suggested that governing bodies should make it possible for their headteachers to develop a mentoring/coaching relationship with someone they respect and trust, probably someone completely independent. This person may be one of the only reliable sources of on-going support for a school leader in a crisis situation, especially if they are suspended.

School leaders who are suspended also need to feel as much as possible like the respected professionals they were before the suspension; after all, suspension is (or should be) a neutral act. Not having access to information and CPD opportunities that would otherwise keep them 'in the loop' can be major blows to professional self-esteem. Anything that can be done to address this – by the individual himself/herself or by others, such as the governing body – should be.

School leaders might also be able to secure advice from HR professionals and other relevant experts, depending on their circumstances and the nature of the situation.

I have suggested to school leaders that were suspended or on 'garden leave' that they also consider taking advice from their own solicitor. Several have done so and found their professional advice and support very helpful. Getting advice that is devoid of emotion is especially important in an otherwise emotionally charged situation.

One head particularly valued help about 'where I stand' and the fact that when she had to submit subject information requests, statements and the like, the solicitor could 'put them in posh, persuasive legalese'. Of course, this help comes at a monetary cost.

One of the unintended consequences (and possible upsides) of experiencing a protracted and complex suspension (or similar) is that the school leader concerned becomes something of an expert on legal, personnel and other relevant matters. Chapter Eight details some of the bits of expertise that one school leader acquired.

Interestingly, one headteacher told me that one of her best sources of support came from her local Safeguarding Team, and that she was very glad that she had cultivated good relationships with the personnel in it over the previous years.

Recovery

As I indicated above, it can be difficult to determine the final phase of a shock-to-the-system event. Not knowing for certain whether it really is the end of the affair makes the whole business of closure challenging. The formal ending (the conclusion of an investigation, for example) doesn't necessarily mean that nothing further will happen.

1. Personal Closure

Still, at some point lines will have to be drawn and decisions of the 'what now?' kind will have to be made. For school leaders at the centre of things, the particular question they will probably need to address is: *'Should I stay or should I go?'*. If they have been through a stressful investigation and cleared of any wrongdoing, they may still feel too bruised or tainted in the 'no smoke without fire' sense to continue headship at their present school. This might also be the case if there has been a serious breakdown of relationships – for example, with the governing body.

The decision is a highly personal one and has to be taken in the light of the exact circumstances and outcomes. For some, the 'right' thing is to stay put with their head held high. For others, it may be right to do this initially but then to move on to pastures new *when they choose to*. The ideal – what makes all the difference for the individual at the level of professional self-esteem and well-being – is not being pushed or pressured but deciding for herself/himself the path ahead.

2. Corporate Closure

If a school community has been through a very difficult or even traumatic experience, then corporate closure and recovery is required. The question the RMLT or equivalent needs to consider or involve the larger school community in deciding is:

What should we do for (i) closure, and (ii) recovery now that the matter appears to have been resolved or has come to an end?

There are three main options to choose from here:

(i) Declare an end to the matter, and maybe have a closure ritual or even a celebratory event.

After a long drawn-out and draining situation, the last thing many schools will feel like doing is having any sort of celebratory event. However, the celebration may be less about securing a 'winning' outcome – there may have been too many costs to consider any outcome an unmitigated triumph – as much as applauding the fact that the staff or school community has stuck together and emerged as possibly stronger and wiser.

It can be salutary to remind staff that destinations are not everything. The educational world has been destination-obsessed for at least two decades – achieving pre-determined objectives as the paramount concern. What experiencing a shock-to-the-system event can tell us is that (i) the destination or goal is not always crystal clear, and (ii) that setting the direction of travel and travelling as one can be more important than arriving at any particular end point. Bearing this in mind, the RMLT leader or school leader might want to say something along the lines of:

'We can't say honestly that we knew where we'd end up, but we were confident that we would get there together. And we have.'

(ii) Let the matter fade away and hope for collective amnesia.

Generally speaking, it is better to acknowledge institutional trauma than to hope that it will dissipate in time or that most staff members will find their own ways of getting over what has occurred. However, at the end of a draining affair there may be little energy or appetite for explicit 'processing' and the judgement might be made to return to some kind of normality with as little fuss as possible.

(iii) Make a very definite decision to learn lessons and ensure the experience is not forgotten.

This response makes most sense in situations where the school has got itself into trouble by its own actions, even if those were the actions of a very few individuals. This has been the response of a number of business organisations in recent years that have 'screwed up' and want to ensure that they don't do so again.

For example, this is what Mary Barra, the CEO of General Motors, had to say to her employees in 2014 after GM was found guilty of putting faulty ignition switches into its cars and causing at least 124 deaths because of it:

'I never want to put this behind us. I want to put this painful experience permanently in our collective memories.'

Fortunately, no school is ever likely to be culpable on this horrendous scale, but the approach – learn, commit to memory and only then move on – is in some circumstances an almost unavoidable one.

Impact Assessment

Though this may need to be done discreetly and in the background so that it doesn't interfere with a return to normal functioning, there are strong arguments for conducting some sort of impact assessment. The key question to address might be:

What have been the effects of the experience on all four quadrants of the Four Quadrant Impact Model?

So we'd be looking here at how individuals have been impacted, both at the external level (their actions, time tables, job effectiveness *etc*) and the internal level (emotions, anxiety levels, motivation, mental focus *etc*). The focus would also be on the impact of the school's systems and operations and perhaps its resources (the 'hard' factors) and at its culture and relationships (the more 'soft' but crucial features of school life at a collective level).

Learning lessons and taking actions

After the impact assessment there will be a number of important questions to address. These might include some or all of the following:

- *What actions do we need to take to address any areas of negative impact?*
- *Would any of the members of staff most directly involved value specialist support (eg counselling)?*
- *Is reputation re-establishment a matter requiring attention? If so, what might be some of the key steps?*
- *Is bridge-building and reaching out something we may need to do?*
- *Has the experience provided surprising benefits or opportunities (eg for Post-Traumatic Growth)?*
- *Are there ways in which our experience and what we've learned from it might benefit other schools and school leaders?*

The ultimate lessons?

I suspect that each school and each school leader will distil its/his/her own ultimate lessons or truths from what they have gone through, but for what they are worth, here are mine:

Control what you can, but you can never control everything. The world is too complex for that.

As you discover the limits of your own autonomy, you will probably emerge a wiser (if sadder) person.

While reality may be too complex and too messy to be governed by a few simple principles, if you seek to operate by a few simple principles (such as Tell Us First and Minimal Necessary Response) then your reality may turn out to be less complex and less messy than it might otherwise have been.

I hope that's a hopeful thought to finish on.

Good luck.

Perspectives from
the front line

What follows are three short chapter-length accounts of the shock-to-the-system experiences of three school leaders. They are intended to add interest, illustrate and make real what I have to say and advise in the body of the book.

The final chapter presents the lessons that one school leader has acquired on the legal side of investigations and the other processes involved when school leaders are suspended. Finally, there is an Appendix which provides details of the Nurture Plan for school leaders referred to in Chapter Three.

Chapter Five: The First Headteacher's Tale

Stopping Bad Things Happening to Good Schools and Good School Leaders – a book title I would have brushed past if I had seen it on a bookshelf as little as two years ago. As an experienced headteacher who has always worked with integrity and never courted controversy, it was not a subject that would have 'reached out' to me.

That was then.....

My professional journey is not an extraordinary one. It is much in line with any other aspiring school leader. A systematic progression from NQT to senior manager, assistant headteacher, deputy headteacher and then headteacher. I worked hard, listened well and learned from my more experienced peers. Whatever the role, I always did my best for the children. I was there to serve.

Three headships in 12 years, six Ofsted inspections, none of them less than 'good' and three of them 'outstanding'. At the time of the devastating, professional bombshell that exploded suddenly in my life, my school had just received an 'outstanding' judgement from Ofsted – moving two grade boundaries from the 'requires improvement' prior to my appointment.

So far so good...

You will read in Mike's book about the dynamics of disproportionality

– molehills so easily becoming mountains, leading to potential shock-to-the-system, school-destabilising events – the 'bad things'.

In my case it was a sudden suspension. I had no inkling of what was about to happen or the effect it would have on me, my colleagues or the school.

What originated as a minor 'concern' that could have been quickly and easily addressed was taken to the 'wrong' person for advice. Rather than following established protocols, the concern was taken to a member of staff who had been waiting for their chance to 'teach the head a lesson'.

I've never been afraid of 'grasping the nettle'. Where there has been an issue regarding performance or conduct I have always acted promptly, preferring not to let a small issue grow or fester. Provided that the discussion is conducted professionally and with honesty, I have always believed it is the right thing to do, both for the staff member concerned and for the children in our care. This doesn't always make you the most popular staff member but the responsibility of headship necessitates action without fear or favour.

Unfortunately, I underestimated the power of a truly determined trouble-maker with their own agenda to pursue. What I didn't know was that the 'determined trouble-maker' had aligned herself with a maverick governor, creating a particularly toxic blend of 'payback and ego'.

I cannot emphasise enough the importance of a mutually professional and positive headteacher/governing body relationship. Neither should the governing body under-estimate the importance of its corporate responsibility for the school. Governing bodies have a huge amount of power and influence and a 'lone wolf' in the pack can be perilous. A head-strong and domineering governor can be difficult to contain in the absence of collective accountability, so beware...

The 'school-destabilising event', or the 'bad thing' that happened to me... the suspension.

From the outset things were poorly managed.

I was visited in school at 4.30 on a Friday evening to be unceremoniously advised of my immediate suspension. No explanation was provided and no procedure or policy document provided (it should never be assumed that a headteacher is super-human and will be able to recall every word of a policy document in the face of profound shock and distress).

The timing of the unannounced visit meant that I was unable to secure any advice from my professional association until the following Monday. It was not a good weekend.

It was some months later before I discovered that the 'maverick' governor had sought minimal advice before deciding alone that I should be suspended. A simple conversation when the concern was first raised would have resolved the issue immediately and without the need for such drastic action. By the time I became aware of this the stack of dominoes had already started to tumble and there was no stopping them until a lengthy and unnecessary process had been followed through to its conclusion.

In my case this was many months later – more of that in a while...

At the point of this fateful meeting I'd had an unblemished career of over 20 years. The simple governing body covenant that Mike references in this book would have been invaluable:

Q. Can I feel assured that you won't forget my service record or treat me as if I had somehow metamorphosed into a quite different person?

Equally, had I been more pro-active in communicating to the governing body issues relating to conduct or performance (the Prevention Management Plan) then the context of the unexpected allegation may have prompted a more considered response prior to determining that suspension was necessary (see Panel 1). This panel and the following panels contain relevant excerpts from the main body of the book designed to avert the kinds of problems I experienced.

Panel 1

'I am addressing the poor performance of X member of staff, so don't be surprised if you hear some grumbles. Just understand that these are actions that have to be taken for the good of the school, even if they create some short-term turbulence.'

Nevertheless, my reality was that I was suspended. From this point on a simple Response Management Plan would have negated most of what followed.

Issue One

At the point of suspension it was unclear to all what the scope of the subsequent investigation would be. This was, quite simply, because of the absence of any real substance to the allegation and the absence of any initial external advice or appropriate reference to policy. Therefore it was not clear what the alleged transgression was.

> **Panel 2**
>
> *Q. Can I be confident that no governor will act unilaterally?*

Issue Two

It took over eight months before I was finally advised of what I was supposed to have done. This was largely due to delays in appointing an investigating officer and an absence of any terms of reference. What followed was an unwieldy investigation with no real focus or substance.

> **Panel 3**
>
> *Q. Can I be assured that your need to address any criticism of me / allegation against me won't mean that you forget my unblemished track-record and everything I have done over the years that has earned your trust and support?*

Issue Three

When I was finally interviewed (some months later), it was by somebody without the prerequisite professional knowledge of the issue. Being the first headteacher investigation that the investigator had conducted it was clear that there was a worrying lack of educational background. Countless hours were wasted explaining technical language and processes which resulted in much of the information provided 'going over the head' of the investigating officer. This led to lengthy delays in the investigation, countless people being needlessly interviewed, relentless requests for documents and, most frustratingly, crucial evidence being lost or destroyed due to a failure in understanding the importance of the documents being referred to.

Any school in this situation must ensure that any investigation is conducted by someone with the appropriate skills to understand what is being presented so that the evidence can be accurately interpreted.

Panel 4

Q. Can I be sure that you as a body will not lose your trust and confidence in me without very good reasons and the evidence for them?

Issue Four

The period of my suspension was a desperately unhappy time. Anyone in a senior role will be able to testify to the emotional and personal commitment involved in leading a school. It is not a job undertaken lightly or without passion. After an unbroken career spanning more than two decades, not going to school on the Monday following my suspension was devastating. What I didn't know was that this would continue day after day for an indeterminable period. When I left the school on that fateful Friday evening, I would not engage in a conversation with any of the staff or my headteacher colleagues for months. The silence was deafening. I am a very pragmatic person and I knew the reasons for my imposed pariah status. It didn't stop it hurting. An agreed covenant would have guided me through the lonely months that ensued.

Panel 5

Q. How will I know that you are still behind me if I am required to be suspended and you are not permitted to talk to me?

In summary form, the covenant the headteacher seeks might express the following sentiments, though not necessarily in the same words:

> '*Can I rest assured that if I'm ever embattled that you will keep faith with me until/unless you have compelling reasons not to, continue to fulfil a duty of care and, if you retain confidence in me, stand up for and by me? I'd like to know that you will keep me and my best interests in mind even when I'm not in sight and/or others turn against me.*'

The professional isolation during this time was probably the hardest thing to cope with. Thankfully, I received invaluable support from my professional association and, with their consent, I also opted to appoint a specialist employment lawyer to advise me –an initially costly intervention, but I knew that I had done nothing wrong and at some point this would be proven. I knew that on this premise, it followed that I would be recompensed for this advice. The advice I received was invaluable, not only for the reassurance it provided but also for its pragmatism and absence of any emotion.

Despite the isolation of my suspension, I was doggedly determined to continue viewing myself as a professional. If the situation was preventing me from carrying out my professional duties I was adamant that it would not stop me *feeling* like a professional.

Reading was my salvation. I devoured every leadership book and academic paper on my bookshelf – those wise words written by others and which the usual pressures of the job leave little time for. I was going to emerge as a wiser and stronger school leader.

The devastating impact of my suspension eventually passed and **recovery** began.

Relationships were largely repaired and my career suffered no long-lasting damage. My story has a happy ending but a little bit of pre-planning would undoubtedly have enabled the happy ending to arrive sooner and with a lot less collateral damage.

The last two years have taught me that no school and no headteacher is immune to bad things happening to them.

In my case, things ended well, with both my career and reputation intact. It didn't end so well for the school. A prolonged headteacher absence, in a school not well-prepared to cope with a crisis, led to unstable school leadership and low staff morale. By the time the light at the end of the tunnel appeared, school performance had plummeted, three-quarters of the school staff had moved on and the school budget was in deficit because of the breath-taking additional costs of process and 'holding the fort'.

I moved on to lead a new school and to forge my new beginning. Those that created the problem 'disappeared'.

The one indisputable fact is that the education of the children in the school suffered during this time. Time the children cannot get back.

Stopping bad things happening to good schools and good school leaders – a capital investment in our children's education that no one can afford to ignore. If it happened to me, it can happen to anyone.

Chapter Six: The Second Headteacher's Tale

Was it over-confidence, complacency, naivety, or just one of those things that couldn't be avoided? It matters because, as teachers, we have been conditioned into always looking for what we could do better rather than blaming others when things go wrong. Generally, I never think too much about whether what I do is right or wrong, having deep and strong values that guide me, instilled in me by altruistic parents. But could this actually have been what let me down?

A phone call, followed by a visit from local authority staff, brought the news that there had been an allegation made about how children had been treated in school. I was sent home while an investigation was carried out and, from there, you could not make it up! Although an intriguing story, I am not proposing to give a blow-by-blow account of what happened. This is mainly because the whole affair has taken up too much of my precious time already and I want to write something positive about it rather than rake over painful memories. As a result, I have set out what I believe are lessons learned.

Television news and the papers, both local and national, as well as social media, were busy for weeks. There was a letter from the MP. Others, who see themselves as the 'great and the good', threw in their ten-penn'orth too. This was particularly exacerbated by the fact that, after a fortnight,

I returned to my post and others who were implicated had remained in post throughout. The reason for this? The allegations were false. Sadly, the 'whistleblower', an ex-member of staff, was not content and pursued every avenue to prove the point, making the whole affair last more than a full, miserable year.

Mistakes were made along the way by absolutely everyone, both inside and outside the organisation and those in authority. It never entered my head that we should plan for such an event and believe me, we didn't! There is little doubt that all my values-driven behaviour was not sufficient to guide me when faced with such obtuse and destructive behaviour, but a plan would have been. So here are some thoughts that might help others should they ever be in a position such as that in which we found ourselves.

When faced with such adversity, each person behaved differently. One of my team held it all inside and became stalwart, another searched for social media comments and read every possible news article and piece of guidance that might be relevant, whilst two of us swung between getting on with our jobs, trying to problem-solve what to do next and, quite frankly, losing it! For my part, I held on to a few key things that no one could take away from me (below) and it is important to search for what these things might be for you:

- My conscience is clear.
- I have a fantastic family.
- I have wonderful friends.
- I've had a great career.

Treat yourself and others to a coach. Don't wait until a problem occurs. You need someone that you know and trust to give your team extra capacity at this time, to temper the radical thoughts and emotions that swamp you and to guide you forward through the mire. Far better this than mopping up crushed and crumpled staff by employing a counsellor after the event, although this may of course still be necessary.

Steven Covey states that 'nothing is as fast as the speed of trust'. Keep this as a mantra for your organisation but do not let it stop you from keeping detailed and accurate school records and getting people to sign on the dotted line when required. In some ways, we had always done this very well but in others we had been lacking.

It is having relationships based on trust that saved our careers and our reputations. Those in governance moved heaven and earth to make sure that everything they did was fair and thorough. They gave up a considerable amount of their own time and tackled some difficult situations. They were fearless when dealing with authorities and the media. They were determined to get it right, whatever the outcome. They were not prepared to settle for an expedient solution and let someone take the fall to minimise bad publicity and appease the whistle-blower. Believe me, this would have been far less painful for all concerned.

It is having relationships based on trust that gave our parents the resolve to stand up publicly for the school and its staff. It was so hard to thank them properly for this because the need for confidentiality meant that we could not share our thoughts. Of course, they didn't do it for thanks, they did it for their children and the school they loved.

However hard it is, maintain the moral high ground and resist the temptation to retaliate or throw any mud whatsoever. You feel frustrated during the event, when you want people to know what really happened, but a whole lot better afterwards when you can say that you didn't compromise yourself, your organisation or your values.

Train your senior staff and governors in media management and think carefully about how much information you share. If you respond to all the media requests, will it satisfy them or make them hungry for more? If you keep issuing the same simple statement saying that things are being dealt with, will they find more devious ways of getting what they want and does that risk inaccurate reporting? In our case, the former applied and we should have shut down our responses to the press sooner. We employed a consultant to help with managing the media and this reduced workload but take care not to use them to drive both what you say and how you say it. You must have overall control.

Train your senior staff and governors in how to manage challenging situations and involve them in making your Response Management Plan. After all, it could be that you won't be there to implement it.

Buy your human resources services from another local authority or private provider. It cannot be healthy for your local authority to be both judge and jury. Luckily we already did and this was another significant factor, as was good access to legal advice and it goes without saying that being a member of a trade union is essential.

Know who your friends are. Actually, what happens is they make sure you know who they are. They will telephone or email you or put their hand on your shoulder at the next meeting you attend. In our case they called in and asked if the writing of a testimonial or supportive statement might help. Remember them if a time comes when they need your support. Turn your experience into something good. Become a trade union advocate for colleagues, share, or just pick up the phone.

Finally, when things are going well, don't become complacent and know for sure that you are naive if you think that it cannot happen to you. However strong the trust within and beyond your organisation and however deep rooted your moral drivers, there is someone out there without too many of them and they can be as unreasonable as they like to create havoc. With a Response Management Plan in place, well-trained leaders and governors and a high-quality coach in arm's reach, there is a life after 'bad things'.

Chapter Seven: The Third Headteacher's Tale

A perfect storm

Sometimes in education (and in life!) a series of events come together at precisely the wrong time and the momentum created causes bad things to happen. It creates a perfect storm. In the 'bad thing' I experienced, there was not one but two (or three) shocks-to-the-system, and they followed hard on the heels of one another. First, there was the sudden and, for the school, the traumatic and mysterious 'disappearance' of the headteacher. Then, almost as soon as I had taken over the headship of this school as well as my own (on a temporary basis and at the request of the local authority) the school was shocked to have a sudden Ofsted inspection seven days into the start of the new school year. The third shock was that the school was placed in special measures.

What made the perfect storm so perfect was a mix of things, some of which could have been prevented or prepared for together with other things that could not have been altered or anticipated, and all converging at the same time.

Not prepared for or predicted

What I could not have anticipated was the early start inspection. Also, although I knew that the school I had taken temporary responsibility for was bereft of a headteacher and probably not in the very best of shape,

I was not personally in the position to have been able to predict the judgement of 'special measures' and the whole new agenda that resulted from this. I'd been told too little about the situation I was going into and I had too little data on the school available to me at an early stage.

Not being able to tell the Ofsted inspector the school's story, and doing the joint learning walk with her, were among the most excruciating moments of my professional life.

The next stage of the situation had also obviously not been planned for: *ie* the need to find the capacity to respond swiftly and decisively to address the perceived shortcomings. A contingent need was that of having to deal with all the psycho-emotional issues of the stakeholders, including shock, disbelief, argument, denial, anger and distress. The challenge of taking the swift decisive action expected of me/the school in this emotional climate had to be balanced by the need to give people a short period of time to accept what had happened.

The other ingredients of this perfect storm included, again very obviously, the absence of the substantive school leader; the drastic diminishing of capacity specifically related to the sudden illness and long-term sick leave of a key member of staff; and the need for me to turn a temporary and limited period of support into a much longer-term commitment, with, as it turned out, collateral damage to my own school. (My few weeks of support ended up being a year.)

But there were also eventualities that could and should have been prevented or prepared for. One of these was easy access to the headteacher's documents. The substantive head had not left any indication of where her passwords could be accessed in an emergency and, since we were not allowed to make contact with her, we had no way of recovering vital information – historic data, lesson observations, monitoring records, staff training logs, behaviour logs – nothing! Another preventable shock was that of staff finding me, not their own headteacher, in the head's office; nothing had prepared them for this.

In terms of the response management phase, there was clearly no LA plan for what had occurred, just a very ad hoc set of responses, including sending in a school improvement partner once the vulnerability of the school had become very obvious, but that was a belated and ineffectual intervention. The LA had no plan for or the funding to support the parachuting in of a 'super head'. There were no guidelines for how I had to respond, other than the need to address the inspection findings and, prior to that, the need to mobilise staff and parents to prepare the environment of the school for the sudden inspection, which both groups did brilliantly. My experience tells me that LAs and Multi-Academy Trusts also need to have plans and procedures for preventing and dealing with bad things happening to schools.

In perfect storm situations, bad things can beget even more bad things. The huge problems that had to be dealt with in the small school I was supporting, compounded with serious capacity issues (only five classes, with three of the teachers – including the deputy – being new to the school), in turn presented huge capacity issues and problems in my own school. In my year's partial absence (I was only able to give it two days a week) it suffered greatly and I believe that it has taken two years to get it back to its pre-support position.

My thoughts and conclusions:

- You can't predict or plan fully for a perfect storm situation, but with better planning you can do more to minimise its likelihood and above all its impact.

- Perhaps all schools should have contingency plans to respond to the situation my own school found itself in – what Mike describes as surge capacity plans.

- When school leaders are 'parachuted' into a school but know too little about the context, then they can unwittingly open all too many cans of worms. Being better prepared by those 'in the know' will minimise the chances of this occurring. It needs to because opening cans of worms can mean getting deflected from agreed priorities and making bad situations even worse.

- Schools and the structures they may be part of (LAs, MATs *etc*) need to think about how necessary information can be exchanged between school leaders (substantive and acting) in the kind of situation I encountered. To use Mike's image, it's about giving thought to the possibility of a drawbridge between those who have and those who have had leadership roles. At the very least, there ought to be protocols in every school to ensure that invaluable information stays in the school and does not disappear with a disappearing school leader. Perhaps that requires school leaders to be regularly 'downloaded' *ie* required to make available to other key members of staff any information they have that is vital for the smooth functioning of the school. (The incumbent headteacher did not return to the school I took over and a compromise agreement meant there was never any communication between us, even to ascertain her welfare.)

- I certainly think that the journey of the 'silent partner' needs to be given a lot more thought.

- In a perfect storm situation, things get worse before they get better. School leaders should prepare stakeholders for this.

Chapter Eight: Top Tips for countering a personal 'Shock-to-the-System' Event

...by a school leader who has learned the hard way

Bad things can happen to good schools and good school leaders – schools and individuals up and down the country can attest to this. However, if you find yourself in the unfortunate position of being on the receiving end of a shock-to-the-system event, then a little bit of procedural knowledge is well worth squirrelling away for a 'rainy day'.

Whilst not professing to have any formal, qualified legal expertise, endless months spent unpicking tricky situations can afford the opportunity of acquiring a layman's collection of useful tips which are offered without liability and in good faith. Please accept them in this spirit. I'm not an expert or pretending to be one, and so I am obviously not liable for any misinformation or advice wrongly interpreted.

1. Policy and Procedure

Read the wording of your School's Disciplinary Procedure carefully. Pay particular attention to the words 'must' and 'should'. Any substantial breaches of stated procedure may render any investigation, hearing or appeal 'unfair'. Procedural failings in terms of published policy and guidance on the part of your employer are unlikely to be viewed favourably by an Employment Tribunal should things reach that stage.

2. Suspension

In certain situations, an employer may decide that suspension with pay is necessary while an investigation is carried out. Suspension with pay should only be used after careful consideration, as a last resort and should be reviewed to ensure it is not unnecessarily drawn out, ie not in place for months on end. It should be made clear that any suspension is temporary, not an assumption of guilt and not a disciplinary sanction. It is also important that your employer makes arrangements for contact to be maintained throughout any suspension.

3. Legal representation

Your professional association will undoubtedly be a good source of support. However, you may also wish to consider commissioning the services of a specialist employment solicitor.

Finding a good solicitor is essential. All solicitors are regulated by the Solicitors Regulation Authority which ensures that strict standards are maintained. Employment law is a complicated field and an area subject to constant change so choose a specialist employment solicitor who will know where to find the most appropriate information for your case. It is useful to select a solicitor who has worked on both sides of employment law – employers and employees – as they will be able to provide a more balanced view of the strengths and weaknesses of your case.

You can find a solicitor or check your chosen solicitor's experience by visiting the Law Society website: www.lawsociety.org.uk.

If you opt to utilise the services of a solicitor, it is vital that you consult with your professional association first. If your union is not in agreement you may lose their support.

4. Advisory, Conciliation and Arbitration Service (ACAS)

ACAS stands for the Advisory, Conciliation and Arbitration Service. They are a government-funded organisation that helps resolve employment disputes. If you find yourself subject to a Disciplinary or Grievance

Procedure make sure you visit the ACAS website. Pay particular attention to the ACAS Code of Practice on Disciplinary and Grievance Procedures.

The ACAS Code of Practice (the 'Code') was issued under section 199 of the Trade Union and Labour Relations (Consolidation) Act 1992 and was laid before both Houses of Parliament on the 16th of January 2015, coming into effect by order of the Secretary of State on the 11th of March 2015.

The 'Code' is an easy-to-read document which employers must pay heed to. A failure to follow the 'Code' does not, in itself, make a person or organisation liable to proceedings. However, an employment tribunal will take the 'Code' into account if your case goes before it. In the event that a judgement is made in your favour and the tribunal feels that your employer has unreasonably failed to follow the 'Code' then any award may be increased by up to 25%. Conversely, if the court feels that you have unreasonably failed to follow the 'Code' they can also reduce any award they have made by up to 25% – so beware!

As with school policies and procedures, pay close attention to the words 'must' and 'should'. A legal requirement in the 'Code' is indicated by the word 'must' and the word 'should' indicates what is considered to be good employment practice.

ACAS is clear in the guidance that whenever a disciplinary or grievance process is being followed, the issues must be dealt with fairly.

Key points to note include:

- Employers and employees should raise and deal with issues promptly and should not unreasonably delay meetings, decisions or confirmation of those decisions.
- Employers and employees should act consistently.
- Employers should carry out any necessary investigations fairly in order to establish the facts of the case.
- Employers should inform employees of the basis of any problem and give them an opportunity to put their case before any decisions are made.

- Employers should allow employees to be accompanied to any formal disciplinary or grievance meetings.
- Employers should allow an employee to appeal against any formal decision made.

ACAS support: www.acas.org.uk/helpline

Latest ACAS guidance and best practice: www.acas.org.uk/modelworkplace

5. Disciplinary investigation

If you find yourself subject to a Disciplinary or Grievance investigation, make sure you visit the ACAS website. The ACAS Conducting Workplace Investigations guidance provides salient advice on how a fair investigation should be conducted.

If a disciplinary investigation is necessary then ACAS expects it to be conducted without unreasonable delay, whilst allowing the employee reasonable time to prepare their case. A fair and logical investigation is the key to everything that may or may not follow.

A clear balance must be struck between the employer's need to gather information for the investigation and the employee's right to be treated fairly and reasonably so that there is no breach of the contractually implied term of mutual trust and confidence.

An investigation should be a fact-finding exercise to collect any relevant information so that an employer can consider the matter and then make an informed decision. If an investigation is necessary, then an employer should act promptly as unnecessary delays may cause memories to fade or give the perception of an unfair process.

Making a decision without completing a reasonable investigation can make any subsequent actions unfair.

The Investigating Officer

The role of an Investigating Officer is to be impartial, fair and objective so that he or she can establish the facts of the matter and make a recommendation on whether or not there is a case to answer. An investigator should do this by looking for evidence that supports the allegation and evidence that contradicts it. It is not an investigator's role to prove the guilt of any party but to investigate if there is a case to answer on the balance of probabilities.

The investigation

When instigating an investigation, an employer should decide what the precise purpose and scope of the investigation will be. An employer must not use an investigation as an excuse to undertake a 'fishing expedition' as this may render it unfair and outside the range of investigations that a reasonable employer should carry out.

An unwieldy investigation or one that does not adhere to good practice could render any disciplinary process unfair. An unfair investigation could include:

- A protracted, lengthy and/or unnecessary suspension.
- A demonstrable lack of fairness and impartiality in the actions of the investigator.
- Breaches of confidentiality.
- A failure to provide details of any allegations and/or evidence in a timely way to enable a fair response.
- A failure to adopt clear terms of reference.

Terms of reference should be created that clearly explain what the investigator's role and responsibilities are for an investigation.

The terms of reference should spell out:

- What the investigation is required to examine.
- Whether a recommendation is required.
- How their findings should be presented.
- Who the findings should be reported to.

It is worth noting that the Court of Appeal has previously decreed that where a misconduct dismissal is likely to result in the loss of an individual's future career in their chosen profession, the investigation, disciplinary process and appeal carried out by the employer must be particularly fair and thorough, and the evidence of misconduct particularly clear and cogent.

6. Grievance

If you are subject to an unfair disciplinary process or believe you are being victimised in some way, you need to consider raising a grievance. If you raise a grievance during a disciplinary process, then the disciplinary process may be temporarily suspended in order to deal with the grievance. However, only raise genuine grievances and do not use a grievance as an opportunity to 'delay' the disciplinary procedure.

If you do raise a grievance related to the disciplinary process, it is likely that both issues will be dealt with concurrently. If your employer fails to address a genuine grievance, it is likely to be viewed unfavourably at a tribunal, particularly if the outcome is likely to affect any decision in respect of disciplinary action.

7. Data protection

Employers owe a duty of confidentiality to all of their employees.

For obvious reasons, maintaining confidentiality is vital in any disciplinary process, particularly if suspension has been utilised. Although a suspension is supposed to be a neutral act, the reality is that if it becomes widely known there will be damage to your reputation regardless of your innocence. It is therefore imperative that the school and investigating officer ensures confidentiality in all matters.

If you suspect confidentiality has been breached, act promptly to address the issue. Tell the investigating officer and your assigned school contact and ask for feedback on any action taken. If the matter is not taken seriously, it may render an investigation unfair. It should also be made clear to employees that any breaches of confidentiality could be viewed as a disciplinary matter.

Breaches of confidentiality may also compromise the integrity of your personal data, so report your concerns to the Information Commissioner's Office (ICO) using their online form.

Subject Access Request (SAR)

If you suspect your employer is withholding information during an investigation or is preventing you from accessing personal information that will assist you in defending yourself, you may need to make one (or several) Subject Access Requests during the course of an investigation or disciplinary procedure.

You may be surprised at how much pertinent and useful information can be sourced in this way!

A failure to respond appropriately to a Subject Access Request should be reported to the ICO. If the ICO investigates your complaint and finds the school to be in breach of the Data Protection Act, this may support your claim of an unfair investigation.

The Information Commissioner's Office website, ico.org.uk, provides lots of helpful information on how to access personal information, including how to submit a Subject Access Request (SAR).

8. Dismissal for Some Other Substantial Reason (SOSR)

This is probably the most difficult part of any **'shock-to-the-system'** event involving a disciplinary procedure.

Imagine you have been through the trauma of an unjustified suspension whilst a lengthy disciplinary investigation has been carried out. At the conclusion of the investigation you are advised that the allegations of gross professional misconduct are not substantiated and there is no case to answer in this respect. However, due to the length of the process and the number of employees interviewed as part of an unwieldy investigation, it is likely that you will be subject to Dismissal for Some Other Substantial Reason (SOSR).

What is SOSR?

The Employment Rights Act 1996 (ERA) gives five potentially fair reasons justifying a dismissal:

- Conduct
- Capability
- Redundancy
- Breach of a statutory restriction
- SOSR – 'some other substantial reason of a kind as to justify dismissal'

SOSR is something of a catch-all, and covers dismissals that are not within the scope of the other four potentially fair reasons for dismissal.

The reason for dismissal under SOSR must be substantial, *ie* not wholly frivolous or insignificant. As long as this standard is met you can be dismissed, *eg* the dismissal of an employee due to an irrevocable breakdown of the working relationship. Your employer could potentially argue that the length and nature of the disciplinary process means that they cannot practically return you to your previous role. Whilst this is not your fault, your employer could say that it is the unfortunate fallout of the disciplinary investigation. It is potentially these circumstances that could entitle your employer to cite 'SOSR' as an alternative to misconduct, albeit your employer could be at risk of a finding of unfair dismissal at a tribunal.

However, despite the potential of being awarded a significant compensatory sum, a tribunal does not have the power to reinstate you and so your dismissal, albeit unfair, would still be on your personnel record.

With this in mind you may decide to consider a 'Settlement Agreement'.

9. Settlement agreements

Settlement agreements can be proposed by both employers and employees, although they will usually be proposed by the employer.

Settlement agreements are legally binding contracts which can be used to end the employment relationship on agreed terms. Their main feature is that they waive an individual's right to make a claim to a court or employment tribunal on the matters that are covered in the agreement. They usually include some form of payment to the employee, a confidentiality clause and a reference.

For a settlement agreement to be legally valid the following conditions must be met:

- The agreement must be in writing.
- The agreement must relate to a particular complaint or proceedings.

- The employee must have received advice from a relevant independent adviser on the terms and effect of the proposed agreement and its effect on the employee's ability to pursue that complaint or proceedings before an employment tribunal.

- The independent adviser must have a current contract of insurance or professional indemnity insurance covering the risk of a claim by the employee in respect of loss arising from that advice.

- The agreement must identify the adviser.

- The agreement must state that the applicable statutory conditions regulating the settlement agreement have been satisfied.

Settlement agreements are voluntary and you do not have to agree to enter into discussions about them.

If you decide to proceed, it is likely to be a process of negotiation during which both sides make proposals and counter-proposals until an agreement is reached, or both parties recognise that no agreement is possible.

The discussions that take place in order to reach a settlement agreement are likely to be on a 'without prejudice' basis. This means that any statements made in a genuine attempt to settle an existing dispute during a 'without prejudice' meeting or discussion cannot be used in a court or tribunal as evidence. This does not apply where there has been any improper behaviour during any discussions, *eg*:

- Harassment, bullying and intimidation

- Physical assault or threatening behaviour

- Any victimisation

- Any discrimination

- Any undue pressure such as not giving reasonable time to consider an offer

- An employer saying before any form of disciplinary process has begun that if a settlement proposal is rejected then the employee will be dismissed

- An employee threatening to undermine a school's reputation if it does not sign the agreement (unless the Public Interest Disclosure Act 1998 applies)

If you find yourself in the unenviable position of having demonstrated your integrity in the face of unfounded allegations but still facing dismissal for SOSR, the right settlement may be worth considering.

Remember – a sizeable compensatory payment could be interpreted as tantamount to an admission of liability by the school. You can also negotiate a good reference which you could not do if your case went to tribunal as the courts have no power to order this.

10. Tribunal

Finally, if you decide to take your case to an Employment Tribunal it is worth knowing that tribunal fees were abolished by the Supreme Court in July 2017. This means that you no longer need to pay fees to make an employment tribunal claim.

If you decide to make a claim to an employment tribunal, an ACAS Conciliation Officer will contact you to see if you want to use ACAS to help try and settle your claim. Settling your claim means coming to an agreement with your employer to stop the case before the tribunal hearing.

If your claim progresses to court, you may wish to appoint a solicitor to represent you. The cost of this can be substantial and there is the risk that you may not be awarded legal costs at the tribunal's conclusion. Therefore, it is worth checking any personal or family insurance policies you have as some include cover for any legal costs which might be incurred in employment disputes. You should ensure that you consider all relevant policies such as buildings/home contents/motor and credit card insurance to see whether any such legal expenses policy exists.

Your Professional Association may also meet your legal costs if your case progresses to a tribunal. However it is worth noting that financial costs may not be borne by your Professional Association if they feel you have refused a fair compensatory offer during any 'Without Prejudice' negotiations.

Finally, whilst negotiating the minefield of different procedures, policies and laws can be daunting, you must:

Keep faith in yourself and your integrity.

- Know that there is help and advice available to support you.
- Remember that if you have done nothing wrong, you have nothing to fear.
- Remember that the law is there to protect you.

***

Information drawn from publicly available sources:

ACAS website (acas.org.uk) for:

- ACAS code of Practice in Disciplinary and Guidance Procedures
- ACAS Conducting Workplace Investigations
- Dismissal for Some Other Reason (SOSR)
- Settlement Agreements
- CAB website (citizensadvice.org.uk) for information on Tribunals

Appendix: A Nurture Plan for your Headteacher?

I've provided training for governors in a number of LAs on the theme of 'Sustaining the Well-being of Your Headteacher'. The training has been very well-received, and I have had a lot of feedback and enquiries on one bit of it in particular: the idea of providing a Nurture Plan for the school's headteacher. Many governors have been in contact to ask what I had in mind by a 'Nurture Plan' and how it might be fashioned.

Even if they were uncertain about what it might consist of, all those governors obviously had a sense that such a thing could be extremely valuable. They were clearly aware that the lot of any headteacher is very demanding and that all manner of events can take a toll on their effectiveness, their well-being and even their health. They picked up on my idea that a Nurture Plan could help to keep their headteacher functioning in optimum effectiveness, and that it could aid the retention and even the recruitment of school leaders.

So what is a Nurture Plan? It's simply a document that sets out the measures a governing body (and possibly, individual governors) agree to take in order to support the flourishing of their headteacher. It's a way of saying that we really value you and want to do anything we can reasonably do to keep you in peak form to lead our school.

It might be triggered by the governing body's concerns about specific, out-of-the-ordinary pressures on the headteacher, or simply done to assure him/her that the governors have his/her best interests in mind. It is clearly better to agree nurture or support arrangements before alarm bells ring.

As I've already indicated, a Nurture Plan or, rather, a commitment to negotiate one, might also be part of a recruitment package put together to attract suitable candidates for a headteacher vacancy.

At a time of severe recruitment challenges, this might well be a compelling reason for a would-be headteacher to choose one school over another.

Talk with your headteacher

Clearly, the drawing up of any Nurture Plan needs to involve the headteacher concerned. If s/he doesn't agree either to having one or to particular components of it, then it will be less than useless; it might even be perceived as an additional burden. The headteacher's input is crucial and, by and large, the content should come from him/her. You, the governing body, might not agree to specific requests, but that's another matter. (For example, one governing body declined their headteacher's request to pay for his gym membership!)

The starting point might be this one general question:

'How can we, the governors, best contribute to your well-being as well as to your effectiveness, apart from doing our job as governors as well and as conscientiously as possible?'

The key thing is to try to provide the kinds of support measures (if any!) that the headteacher would value rather than what you might think would benefit the head. To help him/her think through what forms they might take, you could ask questions such as these:

Q. *How much personal contact do you want with the Chair or with other governors? Would you appreciate contact on a regular (weekly? fortnightly?) basis?*

Q. *Do you want contact to be mainly face-to-face or via email/text messaging or similar?*

Q. *Do you want us, the governors, to confine our contact to school hours?*

Q. Do you want us to be 'on your back' if we think you are working too much?

Q. If not, how would you like us to express our concern?

Q. What kind(s) of support do you most value from us? Emotional/moral support? Practical/hands-on support from governors who have the relevant expertise/resources etc (though we know that our role is not strictly operational)?

Q. How would you prefer us to show our appreciation? For example, verbally? In writing?

Q. Is there anything in particular you would like one or more of us to do, apart from acting like good governors?

Q. Is there anything we are doing that you don't want us to do – that is having or could have a negative impact on you?

Q. What do you need to know, to be convinced about, that could add to your level of well-being? For example: That we will have you in mind in times of particular challenge? That we will step-up-to-the-plate whenever we deem it necessary? That we know that there might be good reasons why you are not always Miss/Mrs/Ms/Mr popular with staff or parents?

Q. Is there anything else for which you would like our backing or that we could make possible for you? For example: Having/not having a regular teaching commitment or having an independent coach or mentor to talk confidentially with.

You might also want to elicit some commitments from your head – his/her part of the 'bargain' as it were. Your head needs to know that any commitments are intended primarily for his/her benefit..

For example:

- That s/he will let you know if s/he is ever under exceptional pressure or being drained by a problem that drags on and on
- That s/he will not try to conceal or minimise any issue of which the GB needs to be aware

Here are parts of two Nurture Plans:

School 1: An 'outstanding' special school

The headteacher's specific requests:

- To continue to receive the emails and texts of support and encouragement from individual governors (who she knew held her in mind), and to continue to feel free to email and text them. She identified what she got from particular governors. For example, she mentioned the wisdom from governor X (a former secondary head), the specialist expertise and advice from governor Y (a former special school head) and the timely 'just the right tone' words of affirmation and encouragement from the Chair.
- To continue to benefit from the services of a coach (me!) for leadership development and the talking through of live issues.

School 2: A 'good' primary school

The headteacher's specific requests:

- That the governors ceased their practice of 'just turning up' and 'popping in'. She wanted the support of particular governors, but as and when she needed it.
- She particularly wanted the GB to back her with parents (specifically, with a group of 'pushy and vociferous' parents) and felt that this would do more than anything else to keep her stress levels down. For example, she asked if the chair would be willing to write to parents requesting them not to email the headteacher directly or, at least, not to send emails (i) late into the evening, and (ii) emails that were long, rude and even threatening.
- She wanted the GB to continue to OK her working at home when she felt that she needed to in order to work on substantial assignments.
- The governors suggested that she might benefit from 'off-loading supervision' with a respected external person, and she agreed to this.

Final considerations:

1. Although governors should take their lead from the head, they may sometimes feel that the head doesn't always act in his/her own best interests, and so should 'support' the head as they (the governors) believe s/he needs to be supported. For example, if the head is clearly a workaholic, then the governors may feel it right to insist that s/he takes steps to address this. This is obviously a tricky and sensitive area, and while some heads may sometimes lack awareness of what they most need to thrive, imposed Nurture Plans are unlikely to succeed, unless the head comes to share this view.

2. Some headteachers need time to 'buy in' to the notion of a Nurture Plan or to be gently persuaded to have one. The reasons behind this vary. Some heads think external support is a sign of weakness or are concerned that others may see it this way. Some heads don't believe that they should benefit in ways that other staff members don't. At a deep level, some reject the idea because they don't think they deserve a Nurture Plan.

3. If there is resistance to a Nurture Plan, then this may be down to the term itself. The GB may prefer to use alternative language – 'maintaining effectiveness', for example, or 'matching to the headteacher's preferences'.

4. Finally, some GBs I've worked with feel that the negotiation of a Nurture Plan or support deal is best worked out initially and in draft between the head and an expert outsider. This can avoid embarrassment and awkwardness (for example, if the head makes it clear who s/he does and doesn't value support from) and ensure it is handled in a neutral but professional way. The GB can then agree or disagree with changes to the Nurture Plan they've come up with.

(MW)